EVERLASTING JESUS

40 Days of Timeless Wisdom for Modern Living

Rick Hamlin

Morehouse Publishing
19 East 34th Street
New York, NY 10016
www.churchpublishing.org

Morehouse Publishing is an imprint of Church Publishing Incorporated.

Cover design by David Baldeosingh Rotstein
Typeset by Westchester Publishing Services

ISBN 978-1-64065-875-2 (paperback)
ISBN 978-1-64065-876-9 (eBook)

Library of Congress Control Number: 2025943757

Printed in Canada

For Will, Tim, and Carol, my beloveds

Table of Contents

Preface

I wrote this book for my friend Anne. She asked me to tell her a little bit about Jesus.

"I'd love get to know him better," she said.

I probably know her husband, Gregg, better than I know her. We were kids in diapers together, so he gets the distinction of being "my oldest friend," or as some people prefer to say, "my friend of longest standing." No one wants to refer to anyone as *old*.

I thought of what Anne said—and kept thinking about it. I do think of myself as a Jesus follower. It's not always easy. I keep trying, and messing up sometimes, but then, I also think Jesus understands that even better than I do. We need to do what we're called to do.

I took a stab at answering Anne's query, digging into the Gospels for examples, putting it down on paper—i.e., the computer. This is what I think it means to follow Jesus. You probably do so already. I just want to be better at it—especially in today's chaotic world. You too?

The Bible quotes are all from the New Revised Standard Version. I'm incredibly grateful for it.

1

LISTEN TO THE OTHER

One of my favorite stories from the Gospels is about Jesus and the Samaritan woman. It's noon. Jesus is tired. He's been traveling, and he's not on his home turf. He's heading back to Galilee, and to do so he must first pass through Samaria.

Samaritans were the *Other*, people who shared some of the same heritage and religious roots as Jesus's people but who were viewed as outcasts. Much like today's social divides, small differences were magnified into barriers. The Samaritans followed the Torah but didn't accept the supremacy of Jerusalem and its temple. They were like estranged relatives—close enough to recognize, but far enough to distrust.

So there Jesus is, in Samaria, passing through. He's thirsty and pauses at the well—Jacob's well, it's called, because it's thought to be on the plot of land that Jacob gave to his son Joseph. Like everywhere Jesus travels, he's in a land rich with heritage and many layers of history. It would be like pausing in Mount Vernon on your way back to Washington, DC.

A Samaritan woman comes to the well to fetch some water, and Jesus says, "Give me a drink." She's taken aback. How could this man, a Jew from Judea, she wonders, ask a Samaritan for a drink—and a woman, no less? Why would he dare flout the strict observances of the day?

In true Jesus fashion, he doesn't respond to the woman with something simple. He invites her into something deeper: "If you knew the gift of God and who it is that is saying to you, 'Give me a drink,' you would have asked him, and he would have given you living water."

God bless this good woman. She doesn't simply nod and smile and hold the thought in her head, silently wondering, *Who is this dude?* She reverts to the obvious, pointing it out to him. He has no bucket, and the well is deep. How is he going to get that "living water"? She pauses to observe just where they are and what a historic spot it is, a place that is crucial to her people.

"Are you greater than our ancestor Jacob, who gave us the well, and with his sons and his flocks drank from it?" she asks.

Now, Jesus is going to tell her who he really is, with a message greater than anyone can imagine. And note that he's telling all this to an outsider, trusting that she might understand it. Outsiders often do. (Note to self: Always consider things from an outsider's point of view.)

"Everyone who drinks of this water will be thirsty again," Jesus says, "but those who drink of the water that I will give them will never be thirsty." How so? "The water that I will give will become in them a spring of water gushing up to eternal life."

This is a picture of true fulfillment—something we long for today. We seek satisfaction in success, relationships, social approval, or material things, only to find ourselves thirsty again. Jesus offers something deeper. The woman wants that water. She doesn't fully understand it yet—but she wants it.

Next up—this is my favorite part—Jesus says to her, "Go, call your husband, and come back." In a way he's setting her up. He knows the truth and wants to see if she'll tell him the truth. Jesus knows *everything* about us, all those secrets we might not want to share with just anybody. That's why it can be so gratifying to pray to Jesus. We don't have to spell it all out. We can trust that Jesus knows what's deepest in our hearts. More important, we shouldn't fudge on the details. He knows the truth that sets us free.

"I have no husband," she says.

"You are right in saying, 'I have no husband,'" he says, "for you have had five husbands, and the one you have now is not your husband. What you have said is true!" In a world where people curate ideal versions of themselves online and hide their true struggles, Jesus invites us to be fully known—and still fully loved.

Anyone passing by would have been shocked and appalled. Shouldn't this holy man be giving his message to a bunch of men instead—upstanding, faithful followers of God—not this unmarried woman with some boyfriend? Why would he stoop so low? Doesn't he realize who she is? (He does indeed.) But then, isn't she, because of her vulnerability, better able to hear him and listen, unlike, say, the arrogant, full-of-themselves scribes and Pharisees? Or unlike me in my arrogant, sure-of-myself moments?

Instead, he goes on to give her one of the most profound teachings in all of Scripture: "The hour is coming when you will worship the Father neither on this mountain nor in Jerusalem. . . . The true worshipers will worship the Father in spirit and truth."

This is the radical relevance of Jesus: worship will no longer be confined to tradition, tribe, or temple. It will be about authenticity—spirit and truth. This kind of worship can happen anywhere, including the chaos of our modern lives.

She replies, "I know the Messiah is coming."

Jesus responds, "I am he." The first time Jesus directly reveals himself as the Messiah—it's not to a priest or a king, but to a marginalized woman from a despised group.

When the disciples show up, they're astonished that he's speaking to her. You'd think that by now they would have known that he wasn't into the power structures of his day. Still, they don't say anything. They're probably trying to take it all in too. The whole thing is so shocking, even if no one says, "Why are you speaking to *her*?"

Then comes a poignant detail that argues for the profundity of what's happening. The woman, transformed, leaves her jar—symbolizing the burdens she came with and the water she thought she needed—and runs to tell others. "Come see a man who told me everything I've ever done!"

Meanwhile, the disciples urge Jesus to eat something. He goes into his mystical beat, saying, "I have food to eat that you do not know about." *What is he talking about? Where is that food? Did someone else bring him something to eat?* You must give the disciples some credit. After all, they're looking after their teacher, their beloved rabbi, and his physical well-being. Somebody needs to do it.

"My food is to do the will of him who sent me and to complete his work," Jesus goes on to say. In today's terms, he's reminding us that true nourishment comes from living with purpose and intention, not just chasing what's easy or expected. What an important message for all of us. Aren't we here at the behest of our Maker, meant to do the work we are called to do? Jesus had a very short time on earth; he was probably in his early or mid-thirties when he died. Those of us who have been given many more decades of life can be grateful to have more time to make our days count.

He then tells his followers: "Look around. The fields are ripe for harvest." That's a message for us, too—there's work to be done, hearts to reach, people to love, right now, wherever we are.

The story circles back to the Samaritan woman, who has now returned with many others. And why? No doubt, she told them how Jesus knew "everything I have ever done."

Jesus. Knows. *Everything.*

REFLECTIONS FOR MODERN LIVING

- Jesus knew her story—and he knows yours. What parts of your story do you hide from others, maybe even yourself? What would it mean to let Jesus into those places?
- Are there barriers—cultural, political, personal—that keep you from seeing others as Jesus sees them?
- Where are you looking for "water" that ultimately leaves you thirsty?
- What does it look like, in your life, to worship in spirit and truth—not just on Sundays, but in your everyday moments?
- What is the "jar" you could leave behind to follow the deeper calling of Jesus?

2
INVEST IN YOURSELF

The wonderful thing about Jesus's stories—parables, as they're called—is that you can find in them multiple meanings. Jesus is speaking to multiple people, sometimes large crowds. The messages are for all of us and at the same time just for one of us. *What? Me, Jesus? How did you know that about me?*

Forgive me if these reflections seem shamelessly personal. Unabashedly, I share them in the hope, the reassurance, the belief that something here might click with you. Why follow Jesus? Easy enough—it's where true goodness lies, and with it joy, courage, and clarity for today's chaotic world.

Let's look at the story he tells about the talents (the source for our use of the word today). Back then, a talent was a unit of currency. Some scholars say one talent was equal to twenty years of wages; others estimate it more conservatively, a thousand bucks per talent, say, or maybe more. No matter, it was a significant sum. And in the story Jesus tells, the master heads off on a journey and entrusts his slaves, his unpaid workers, with all his property, including money. To one he gave five talents, to another he gave two talents, to the third he gave only one talent.

You wonder if this guy had figured out something in advance and was doing a little test. Perhaps he gave five talents

to the one who was the most talented—to use a word—and deserved it the most. He then gave two talents to the one who was a little less talented, and the fellow who only got one talent, well, he wasn't top drawer. Indeed, there is something felicitous in English about the very word. Talent is a gift, it's what we do well, it's how we market ourselves, it's what we share with the world.

The three who were entrusted with the money made different choices. The one who had five talents invested the money wisely, taking a risk, so that he ended up with five talents more. Pretty impressive. The one who was given two talents did something similar, ending up with two talents more. But the one with one talent went off and dug a hole and buried it, hiding the money from anyone who might steal it, or maybe from his own instinct to spend. If the coin was buried, no one would touch it, including him.

We get a very clear picture of this guy. He's afraid. He doesn't trust his boss, nor does he trust himself or anyone else. He can imagine all sorts of terrible things happening and gives himself over to those dreadful fantasies. He must have shivered in terror all the while his boss was gone, doing nothing for himself, caring little, in fact, for himself. And fear, unchecked, is the great thief of purpose in every generation.

The boss is away for a long time, feeding the fears of those he had entrusted with the money. *Where had he gone? Would he ever return?* Imagine all the terrible things that could have happened to the man. What if he died while he was gone? Surely, his heirs would be breathing down their necks, demanding every cent the man had given them—and then some.

The boss or master does return and calls the three to his lair to settle accounts. Worker number one comes forward. What did he do with the five talents he was given? You can imagine his pride as he steps forward, with a hefty money bag. He made five talents more with what he was given. *Well done, good and trustworthy slave*, he is told. Trustworthy—note that word. Think of the trust we invest in those who do good works with whatever we—or the good Lord—might have given them. "You have been trustworthy in a few things," his master tells him. "I will put you in charge of many things. Enter into the joy of your master." Then again, hasn't he already savored some of that joy? His faith in his gifts—his talents—served him well.

Next comes slave number two. "Master," he says, "you handed over to me two talents," and then shows him the fruit of his labor. "I have made two more talents."

"Well done, good and trustworthy slave. You have been trustworthy in a few things. I will put you in charge of many things. Enter into the joy of your master." He gets the same accolade his colleague got.

Lastly, the terror-stricken fellow with the lone talent comes forward and reveals who he is in relationship to his master—surely, we're also meant to see how it is his relationship to God. Fear only begets more fear. "Master, I knew you were a harsh man, reaping where you did not sow, and gathering where you did not scatter seed, so I was afraid. I went and hid your talent in the ground. Here you have what is yours."

When we think the worst of people, we often find our projections fulfilled. "You wicked and lazy slave!" he is told. "You knew, did you, that I reap where I did not sow and gather where I did not scatter?" Jesus was speaking to an audience for whom those agricultural terms would have meant a lot. We hear them as metaphors; to his hardworking, living-off-the-land listeners, they would have been more vivid. Reaping where you did not sow and gathering where you did not scatter is the behavior of a cheater. That's the cautionary wisdom here: don't bury what you've been given. Don't let fear, insecurity, or perfectionism keep you from showing up.

"Then you ought to have invested my money with the bankers," he goes on to say. "And on my return I would have received what was my own with interest." That's a term we're more likely to understand, accustomed as we are to seeing interest rates posted left and right. Still, this would have shaken up Jesus's largely Jewish audience, who knew from the Hebrew Scriptures that they weren't supposed to loan money for interest—as if that's all Jesus is talking about.

The boss commands the others to take the one talent away from the man and give it to the one who had had the ten talents. Then we get a line that stands alone. "For to all those who have," the master says, "more will be given, and they will have an abundance. But from those who have nothing, even what they have will be taken away."

Mind you, the words are coming from a character in a story—just in case you thought the line would justify any greedy financial decisions and some self-congratulatory backslapping. *Didn't I earn it? Can't I keep it?*

How easy it is for those of us—including myself—who had much given to us in childhood, including loving and encouraging parenting, to claim that any accomplishment of note was something we did ourselves, to our credit. We like to think we deserve our riches because we made every cent ourselves.

The poor fellow with the one talent comes to an unfortunate end, thrown into the outer darkness, where there will be "weeping and gnashing of teeth." That sounds dramatic, but I think it's symbolic. When we don't live fully, when we let fear rule us, we do feel cut off—disconnected from joy, from meaning, from others.

When you hear a Jesus story it's a little like hearing the work of some great composer and asking what one little note means. The great composer answers the question by playing the whole piece over again. The meaning of the story isn't one single phrase: it's the whole thing. Listen, take it in, ponder over it, ask yourself, "Why, Jesus, why?"

The modern takeaway: Don't live in fear. Don't let fears dictate your behavior. It will only bring on fearful results. Live in hope. Take risks. Trust in God. Invest in yourself, as Jesus invests in us. Let your life be a bold offering, not a buried coin.

I don't think this is a template for investment bankers or stockbrokers of today. It's about spiritual riches and emotional gifts as much as anything. No matter what you're given—and the various results can be confusing if not seemingly unfair—invest it in the worthiest calling and the richest serving. The word "slave" can be jarring, as well as the word "master," but think about it: We can make ourselves slaves to monstrous things and raise the demonic to the role of master in our lives. Or we can be slaves to exactly what grants us freedom: God's infinite love. Our talents are worth the best. Serve *that* master.

Reflections for Modern Living

- What "talents" or gifts—spiritual, creative, practical—have you buried because of fear or doubt?
- What would it look like to "invest in yourself" with trust in God today?
- Are you waiting for the perfect conditions to act—or is it time to step out in faith, however imperfectly?
- What might you create, offer, or become if you trusted that God's joy is already available to you?

3

Find Jesus in others

The world is made up of sheep and goats—or maybe I should say *sheep vs. goats*. There will come a time, Jesus says, when the Son of Man in his glory sits on a throne and divides the people into sheep and goats, one or the other. The heavenly King will decide. (And remember it's a story. Jesus is telling another story.)

Sheep and goats, really? It seems monstrous, if not unfair, that there would be such a division, as though we had any choice in the matter. But then again, maybe we do. We choose every day whether to see others with compassion or contempt, whether to serve or turn away.

First off, what would be wrong with being a sheep or a goat? I like them both. I drink goat milk and savor sheep yogurt (taking advantage of the health benefits of both). The distinction or comparison seems vague to this twenty-first-century city dweller. But it would be immediately apparent to Jesus's listeners in first-century Judea. They saw the reckless goats scrambling over rocks. They watched over sheep in the fields. Sheep were docile, gentle, biddable creatures; goats could be feistier. Sheep were considered easier to raise, responding to the calling of their shepherd.

In Jesus's words, the King, as he calls this decider, determines the fate of both. The good people, the sheep, go on the right, the goats go to the left. The former are granted life everlasting, sublime pastureland with nary a storm cloud in sight—or maybe it's just that the clouds are welcomed for all their benefits to the landscape. The goats are banished into some sort of eternal punishment, a future of unescapable misery. It's also possible that the two are in the same place and just see things differently. As the old saying goes, hell is being in heaven and not liking it.

One caveat: When you hear of life everlasting or eternal life in the Scriptures, and also eternal damnation, be careful where your imagination takes you. It's easy enough to figure heaven is somewhere above the clouds where angels play harps and people float around in bliss rather than burn in a fiery tomb underground, demons throwing darts at them and stabbing them with knives. When you linger with Jesus's words you start seeing—or rather, feeling—something different. This life eternal is much more an emotional and spiritual state that starts here on earth. We get to be like sheep, cared for and loved, in constant community, close to the shepherd at hand. We do all the right things, effortlessly.

And what exactly do we do to deserve it? Keep reading.

When Jesus or God or the Spiritual One was hungry, as he tells it, we gave him food. When he was thirsty, we gave him something to drink. When he was alone and away from home, we welcomed him into our home. When he was without clothes, we gave him something to wear. When he was sick, we cared for him. When he was in prison, we visited him.

When we hear this, we might scratch our heads—as Jesus's listeners certainly did—and wonder, "When did we do all these things?" We don't remember. When did we see our Lord hungry and give him food? When did we see him thirsty and give him something to drink? When was he alone and we took him into our house? When was he without clothes and we gave him something to wear? When was the Lord sick or in prison and we visited him? When did we act like sheep and not goats? All those "whens"!

Goodness has its own inscrutability. Perhaps because those who are good—when *we* are good—have such pure motivation. We don't harbor any self-congratulatory accolades. The truly good ones are not going around saying, "Aren't I great? Didn't I give a great presentation? Wasn't I generous? Did you see me visiting that friend in the hospital?" They just do good because they do. Happiness doesn't have to proclaim itself. Heaven is here on earth. Or to repeat that saying, hell is being in heaven and not liking it.

The King in the story, or God, or Jesus, the sublime Whoever, answers that slew of "when" questions, that whenever we did those good things, we did them *for* Jesus, to Jesus. However, when we *didn't* do them, when we ignored the world's misery, when we didn't see that the sick, the lonely, the imprisoned, the hungry, the thirsty, the poorly clothed needed our help, we missed seeing who they really were. We missed seeing God on earth.

At our worst, we're sent away to a place of eternal punishment where people burn forever. There is a hell on earth, which they or we have unwittingly claimed. We can be ornery goats, not biddable sheep.

The choices seem very clear then, don't they? We're expected to feed the hungry, clothe the naked, give shelter to the homeless, visit the sick, send them emails, call them, and spend time with the prisoners, including those who find themselves imprisoned in inner torment. Looking for Jesus here on earth? Turns out that the Lord isn't so far away after all. Look around you. See the opportunities to serve him.

I must confess that when I do those good things, it usually takes an elbow nudge or two: "Come on, Rick, you're not doing anything this Saturday, volunteer at the church soup kitchen," or "Okay, Rick, you've been in the hospital before. You know how much it meant to have visitors in that lonely misery, drop on by. Just show up. If they don't want to see you, you'll find out. You might be surprised." When the beggar holds out his cup to me, when the woman on the subway gets close enough that I can smell her, I don't see Jesus, not until I drop a coin or a buck in the cup or in the open hand. And then, even in this shamelessly secular era, they always say, "God bless you." I think I'm meant to take them at their word.

Because Jesus is there. Jesus is right here. Right now. All around us. In need. In love. Waiting to be seen.

Reflections for Modern Living

- Where have you seen someone in need—and looked away? What might it look like to respond instead?
- How might your daily routine change if you truly believed Jesus was present in every person you meet?
- What does "eternal life" mean to you—not just after death, but here and now?
- Who in your life today is imprisoned—by grief, by fear, by loneliness—and needs your visit, your call, your kindness?

4

Love your enemies

It's easy to love the people who love us. But Jesus tells us to love those whom we perceive as enemies. "Love your enemies," he says. Why is that?

I believe it's because we need to know that side of ourselves.

In today's polarized world—where we follow echo chambers, block dissenting voices, and reduce people to headlines—Jesus's call is more urgent than ever. We're expected to choose sides, believe certain narratives, and reject "the other." Today, we can construct a world where we only hear one side, only get news links from sources who think like us, only log on to that authority that we've decided we can trust. How do we know we can trust them? Easy enough. They seem to like what we like and hate what we hate. Facts are supposed to speak for themselves. But what about the people who are delivering the facts?

I remember my aunt, a conservative Goldwater Republican, telling me that she thought it was important to read multiple news sources, to hear both sides. Did she do that? Possibly. But bless her heart for conceiving of the mere possibility and telling me so. Her openness to hearing both sides is something we desperately need today.

This is not just a political matter but also an emotional and spiritual one. We must love our enemies because we, too,

are capable of being enemies. We all have a dark side. We can be greedy, proud, vain, hateful, petty, arrogant, intolerant, uncompassionate, niggling, prejudiced, stubborn, and unremittingly blind to all those faults. "I'm a good person, aren't I?" we tell ourselves. "At least I'm better than that person. Just look at me."

Yes, look at you. Look closely. Look deeply. There is a reason for the word "sin" in our vocabulary of faith. There is a reason that Jesus says, when giving his prayer to the disciples, one we say again and again to this day, that we are to ask God to forgive our sins as we forgive the sins of others. That language in the Lord's Prayer, or the Our Father, as it is also called, can be confusing with the various translations: "Forgive us our debts as we forgive our debtors" or "Forgive us our trespasses as we forgive those who trespass against us" or "Forgive us our sins as we forgive those who sin against us." It's all the same. How can we begin to forgive others if we don't look deep into ourselves and confront our own wrongs?

What we often do—what I do (yes, you do, Rick, *you* do!)—is avoid confronting the darkness and instead project it on others. To put it in Jungian terms, we project the shadow self. The inner dialogue can go something like this: "That guy is so arrogant, so sure of himself. He's always talking, bragging, dominating the conversation." "That woman is so critical of everybody, gossiping about this and about that, looking down on the world as though she knows everything." And you, Rick, and you? Do you ever do things like that?

I find it telling that the one person who drives me nuts at church, the one I dread being with on any committee or in any group, is the fellow who is—truth to tell—a lot like me. In fact, he talks almost as much as I do. Goes on and on. *Forgive me, Lord, for my arrogance, always being so sure of myself.*

There is a reason Jesus urged his followers to stick together. There is a reason we, his followers, find ourselves in churches or twelve-step groups, in Bible studies or prayer groups, in person or on Zoom. How else do we see how much we need to forgive and to be forgiven? If we're being truly honest, the protective walls of self-congratulation and self-adulation will come tumbling down. We can't really love until we learn to love what seems so unlovable, not just in others but in ourselves.

It is so much easier to remain in separate guarded camps: them versus us. Monstrous "them" versus saintly "us." Be aware, intensely aware, when you start casting aspersions. Is it really the other, or is it also you? Believe it or not, it can be a lot of fun to hate, to boil over in self-righteous anger at those people who promulgate seemingly terrible ideas and preach all sorts of gospels to prove their higher moral ground. But has your hatred blinded you to any truth they might be offering or prevented you from even seeing who they are, denying you any sort of compassion? If you find a way to love them, you might also find a way to better love yourself. If you love those who love you, as Jesus says, what credit is that to you? Dig deeper. Love your enemies. And that's just for starters.

Jesus went on to say that we are to pray for those who persecute us, "that you may be children of your Father in heaven." I often shrug my shoulders when I hear that sort of holy language. Persecute? Who would be persecuting me? I'm such a good guy, generous, thoughtful, kind, understanding. However, if I read enough angry screeds on the internet, I can indeed discover that some people use language that is meant to persecute me—yes, good old me. Is it no wonder that we avoid having to confront such possibilities? After all, why read someone who is so terribly wrong and ill-informed? Why read anything hateful?

Encouraged to hate, can't we love instead?

To pray for others, as Jesus asks us, is to rediscover that compassionate nature we are all given. Think of the possibilities. If I'm intent on praying for peace and living in a world that is imbued with peace, it can only come when I understand the other side—in others and myself.

To love your enemies is not to excuse injustice—it's to resist the cycle of hate. It's the first step toward peace.

Reflections for Modern Living

- Who have you written off as an "enemy"? What might happen if you prayed for them by name?
- When have you seen your own faults in someone else—and judged them instead of relating?
- What do you fear would happen if you tried to understand the "other side"?
- How might loving your enemies free you to love yourself more deeply?

5

Celebrate the Milestones of Life

Jesus's turning water into wine at the wedding in Cana is often described as one of the first miracles Jesus ever performed. One of my favorite Bible stories (no wonder), it has been vividly portrayed by artists over the centuries. My favorite depiction is the vast painting of the scene by the sixteenth-century artist Paolo Veronese, which fills a wall at the Louvre Museum. I saw it for the first time on one of those stay-in-cheap-hostels Eurail tours through Europe. I could have stood there for hours—bypassing the crowds huddled around the *Mona Lisa*—gazing, celebrating, feasting with the wedding guests, looking up at Jesus, wishing for a glass to drink myself, cheap at the price.

Jesus sits at the head of the table, where you might expect to see the bride and groom. The guests are having a wonderful time, most of them oblivious to the miracle worker in their midst. Why should they notice? They have good wine to drink, a marriage to celebrate, lavish clothes to admire, friends to chat with, music to listen to. Isn't that so often how miracles happen—quietly, while life unfolds around them?

I can imagine a complaint or two about the historical inaccuracy of the clothes they are wearing, anachronistic and too grand. These aren't first-century Judeans in the backwater of the Roman Empire, but portraits of distinguished people of another era, a king, a queen, an emperor, a poet, a cardinal, a statesman, musicians. One of them is thought to be the painter himself. (Why not place oneself into the picture, into a sublime moment with Jesus?)

They're dressed in silks and satins, headdresses and robes—attire that would be worn at a sixteenth-century party, one that Veronese might have attended. *Didn't he know what people wore back in Jesus's time?* you might wonder. Of course, he did. He was as historically informed as any of his educated contemporaries. He was making a not uncommon artistic choice, one that offers a compelling insight. It's as though he's saying: What if that miracle happened here, in grand Renaissance architecture with a balustrade like something in one of our palaces? What if people like us were there, dressed in our best?

The story as it goes: Jesus and his disciples had been invited to a wedding in Cana in Galilee. Mary, his mother, was there, too, and when the wine gave out, she gave the word to Jesus: there's no wine (as if he didn't already know). It's a little shocking to hear how Jesus addresses his dear mother, saying, "Woman, what concern is that to you and to me?" Then he goes into a mystical vein, adding, "My hour has not yet come." Is he really trashing his mom? I think not. As always with Jesus, he's intensely aware of his listeners and uses every chance to make a point. *Woman, what is that to you?* What is that to all of you? Does it matter that there's no wine to drink? Does the party have to stop now? *Tell me.* Say it, know it, don't just mutter it under your breath.

Okay, we want a party! We want to celebrate. We need *more* wine. Please, Lord, please.

My favorite line in the story then comes from Mary—she, who more than anyone so far, knows what he is capable of. "Do whatever he tells you," she says to the servants. The Mother Mary sounds like many a proud mom. *Do what my kid says.*

Gospel stories don't mind getting technical, giving exact numbers. It turns out there were six stone water jars, each capable of holding some twenty or thirty gallons (one can be grateful to Bible translators who put such measurements in modern terms). The water would be there for the Jewish rites of purification, another reason the writer can put down those figures with confidence. A good miracle story should have some solid numbers behind it, like the five loaves and two fishes that would feed five thousand (we'll come to that).

Jesus tells the servants to fill the jars with water, and they do, up to the brim. Next step? He tells them to take some out and give a sip to the chief steward. Note: There's no magical ceremony where Jesus stirs the water or raises his hand to squeeze some mystical grapes. Jesus isn't into Vegas-style showboat stardom. This is a wedding, presumably a modest one if it happened in Galilee (unlike the lavish Veronese painting). Apparently, they hadn't stocked enough wine for the guests to celebrate.

Here comes the ultimate taste test. The wine expert takes a sip and savors it, clueless to where it had come from. He deems it an excellent vintage. He's also something of an expert on what happens at parties. Most hosts, as he says, serve the best wine first and the second-rate stuff later, after everyone has gotten drunk. But no, here they've kept the good wine until now.

Take this how you wish. The metaphorical subtext seems unavoidable. Jesus, the Messiah, has finally shown up. The good wine is here at last.

Today, religion often gets a bad rap. Many now believe that it's all about denial and self-sacrifice, exercises of fasting and self-discipline. And, to an extent, that's true, and Jesus will explore that. But he's also one to stress the dire necessity of celebration and joyous community. Give up the dour expressions at the gate. To be a follower of Jesus is to savor those opportunities to be together with loved ones and strangers. Gather around a table to eat and drink. The ritual he gave his followers on the night before he died, to break bread, to drink wine, is the ultimate example, one that I follow with delight. That it's done in community is especially important. Research has often shown that a gathering of minds is far more creative than what one lone soul can produce. Good things come of togetherness. That's a reason to celebrate. Drink the wine that came of mere water, transformed by God's love on earth. Don't save the best for last.

Reflections for Modern Living

- Where in your life have you failed to notice a quiet miracle because you were too busy or distracted?
- How do you celebrate with others—and what might it look like to make joy a spiritual practice?
- Is there a "water-into-wine" transformation happening in your life that you haven't yet recognized?
- How can you make space this week to gather with others, enjoy good things, and honor God in the celebration?

6

FOLLOW SCRIPTURE CAREFULLY AND JUDICIOUSLY

I have tremendous admiration and respect for those good people who can quote the Bible, chapter and verse, at the drop of a hat. Alas, I'm not one of them. I read Scripture every day, but the only time I can pull up a quote—without doing a Google search or thumbing through pages of the Good Book—is if it's something I've sung. The words linger longer in the brain when they've been set to music. No wonder the psalms were all sung for millennia before they were ever just read—as we more often do—from the printed page.

It's tempting to use a Bible quote to justify certain choices in life or one's behavior. Why not? Isn't that what we're meant to do? Isn't that what I'm doing here? (Dear reader, this is when you can decide to stop reading.) And didn't Jesus do that? But then, didn't those who differed from Jesus turn to Scripture to argue with him and show everyone else how wrong he was? Wasn't Scripture the perfect last word?

Jesus grew up in a rich Jewish culture, inculcated in the faith of generations of Judaic followers. He might have been

born in a stable, celebrated by lowly shepherds, visited by wise men from the east, but on the eighth day he was circumcised like any Jewish boy and was brought to the temple in Jerusalem, where his parents offered a sacrifice: a pair of turtledoves (another indication of their poverty; turtledoves would be one of the cheapest options).

As the book of Luke also tells us, his parents took him to the temple in Jerusalem again, like good observant believers. When he was twelve, they made the sacred journey. They were heading back home and had traveled for a day before they realized they'd missed him (obviously they were not alone on the journey). Frantic, they looked among the relatives and friends traveling with them. In the end, they returned to Jerusalem and searched high and low. They found him at the temple, this twelve-year-old boy stunning the scholars and teachers with his knowledge and wisdom. Not for nothing would he be called Rabbi by his followers—Teacher.

Some scholars have suggested that he was illiterate, as might be expected of the son of a carpenter, and that he could only quote so well from Scripture because he grew up hearing it in the synagogue. I don't believe that. Neither do others. The Jewish culture was extraordinarily literate, as at the heart of their faith were books of the Bible that had been passed down through the centuries and read from scrolls in the synagogue.

These texts were largely recorded in Hebrew so that we often refer to them as the Hebrew Bible. One of the miracles, though, behind the spread of Christianity was something that happened in the third century B.C. with the Septuagint, the translation of the Hebrew Scriptures into Greek. At the time of Jesus's birth, few people could speak Hebrew, and even fewer could read it. Greek was the common language, and Aramaic was what was most widely spoken among the Jewish community. (I have a former colleague who grew up in a Syrian Christian family, one of the oldest branches of Christianity. I loved to hear her recite the Lord's Prayer in Aramaic.)

To leap ahead, one of the reasons Christianity could spread around the Roman Empire was that there was this way to look back at the Hebrew Scriptures and read them, hear them, in a language most people could understand. Monotheistic Judaism, in contrast to the many deities in the Greek and Roman pantheons, appealed to many Gentiles—"God lovers," as they were called. When the Apostle Paul was reaching out to communities of believers in Rome, Corinth, and Galatia, he could confidently quote from the Hebrew Scriptures, using the Greek, confident that the recipients of his letters would understand his references. Mind you this was 1,500 years before the Bible was ever broken up into chapter and verse, Scripture's own Google-search mechanism.

In the Gospels, Jesus makes frequent references to Scripture, sometimes referring to a story or personage, like Jonah and the fish or Solomon and the Queen of Sheba. He talks about Scripture like the "book of Moses," where you can read about the burning bush. When he gives a sermon in the synagogue of his hometown of Nazareth, he unrolls the scroll and reads from the book of Isaiah. He makes frequent references to the commandments, like when he interacts with the rich young man who is only too confident that he has followed the commandments. Jesus even prays the Scripture, most poignantly when he was on the cross dying and was heard to say, in Aramaic, "Eli, Eli, lema sabachthami?" or "My God, my God, why have you forsaken me?," a direct quote and reference to Psalm 22, verse one. I sometimes wonder if maybe he even sang it, the way it would have been sung in a synagogue.

If Jesus could so fervently pray, turning to Scripture, digging deep into his soul, can't we? Of course!

Scripture is this incalculable, timeless gift we've been given, an enormous boon to our faith. When we're struggling, when we're learning, when we're helping someone, when we're arguing with others or arguing with ourselves, when we're looking to grow, we have it right there, an eternal guide, chapter and verse. Like I said, I read Scripture every day, a few psalms in the morning as I sit down for breakfast, then passages from the New and Old Testaments. Do I do it out of holy obligation? Goodness, no. I do it to help myself. As I've said before, the world's news—most of it alarming—can wait. Better to set my heart right with a piece of the Good News. First things first.

What you always get from Jesus is that it's not simply about spouting off verses of Scripture to justify your behavior, but rather about truly living it. Let's look at something that happened early in his ministry. Before he even launched what he had come to earth to do, to teach and serve, he spent forty days and forty nights in the wilderness, fasting, something we commemorate annually in the spiritual calendar, marking those forty days before Easter (skipping Sundays) as the season of Lent. As a spiritual reminder, people often choose to give up something for those forty days (and usually on Sundays too), like that glass of wine before dinner or some tasty chocolate dessert. (Someone I know and love found that when she gave up chocolate for Lent, she actually gained weight by eating so much else to make up for it. Ha.)

I don't drink wine, and the chocolate I eat doesn't have much sugar in it, so I find it more honorable to make a Lenten practice of trying to give up something like self-congratulations or selfish smugness or take on something, like a charity, that I care about and pray for. What must have been a huge penance to Jesus was being there in the wilderness for forty days and forty nights, without any followers or any friends. How lonely. Hungry and alone, no wonder he could be tempted by the devil.

This is where we see Scripture being used for good and then misused in a manipulative fashion. As the devil tempts him, Jesus responds by quoting Scripture. "It is written," Jesus says, "'One does not live by bread alone, but by every word that comes from the mouth of God'" (Deuteronomy 8:3).

Take note of how the devil fights back, taking Jesus to Jerusalem and putting him—talk about manipulation—on the pinnacle of the temple, the tempter making his own argument using Scripture. If Jesus is the Son of God, he should be able to throw himself down with no danger. After all, it is written, "He will command his angels concerning you" and "On their hands they will bear you up, so that you will not dash your foot against a stone," the devil quoting Psalm 91, verses 11 and 12. Jesus comes back with more from Deuteronomy: "Again it is written, 'Do not put the Lord your God to the test'" (Deuteronomy 6:16), the two of them using Bible verses to argue.

Finally, Jesus is taken to a high mountain and shown all the kingdoms of the world with all their splendor. "All these will I give you, if you will fall down and worship me," says the devil. In an instant Jesus could have the devotion of the whole world, if he would just worship Satan. Isn't that the sort of temptation put before all of us, the lure of money, wealth, and power?

Jesus puts an end to it, with one final quote. "Away with you, Satan," Jesus says, "for it is written, 'Worship the Lord your God, and serve only him'" (Deuteronomy 6:13). Satan leaves and the angels come and comfort Jesus, a reminder to me that Jesus is not about worldly power but something far deeper and larger.

The whole scene is a compelling drama. What a way to start things off! When I read it every Lent, I can hear myself along with Jesus arguing with the strongest language possible, the words recorded in Scripture. But you can't look at the story without also noting how the devil does the same. The devil is wrong, and Jesus makes that clear. Scripture is powerful, Scripture is true, but even Scripture can be misused in the wrong hands. What's more important is to hear the intent behind the words. That's what informs Jesus's choices of Bible verses, as he refutes the devil's arguments.

Does evil exist in the world? Are there not devils looking to distract us and lead us astray? Indeed, there are. The Bible is a powerful ally to turn to for help—even today, thousands of years after its compilation. Doing so, I pray for understanding and compassion. I don't want to find myself in the power of ones who use Scripture manipulatively. May they be banished, as Jesus banished them, the angels coming to our care. The largest message is God's love, seen in Jesus himself.

Let me end with the way Jesus puts it. "You search the scriptures," he says, "because you think that in them you have eternal life; and it is they that testify on my behalf. Yet you refuse to come to me to have life" (John 5:39–40). I come to Jesus not just for words but for life.

REFLECTIONS FOR MODERN LIVING

- Do you turn to Scripture for guidance—or only to prove a point? What's your true intention?
- When have you seen Scripture used to hurt rather than to heal—and how did you respond?
- What Bible verse or passage has personally shaped you? Have you returned to it recently?
- In what ways can you let Scripture form your life—not just your opinions?

7

Welcome the Latecomer

When Jesus manages to tell a story that gets you all riled up, you know that's exactly what he's after. You can't just walk away saying, "Oh, that's nice." You can't dismiss it either. It's Jesus. He's got something to say. He wants to change our behavior. He gets under our skin. This is the one that whenever I hear it—read it—I always think, "That's not fair." But then remember what the late Jimmy Carter said all those years ago? "Life's not fair." Is it? Or isn't it?

As the story gocs—and rcmember it's a story, not a historical account—the landowner goes out early in the morning, shortly after dawn, I suspect, to hire laborers for his vineyard. They agree on what they'll get paid, the usual wage for a day, and he puts them to work. A little later, at nine o'clock, he sees more workers standing around idle and offers them work, promising to pay whatever is right. He does it again at noon, and then around 3:00 p.m. As late as five o'clock there are more laborers hanging out, doing nothing. "Why are you standing here idle all day?" he asks. No one has bothered to hire them, they say. He sends them into the vineyard to work.

When evening comes, it's time to pay all the workers. He tells his manager to call them forward, starting with the last laborers and ending with the first. The ones who were hired at five o'clock get the full daily wage, even though they worked the least. When the ones who'd been out there laboring in the hot sun all day long come up, naturally they expect they'll get more. No, they receive the same amount, a day's wage, exactly what had been promised them. They complain out loud—wouldn't you? It isn't fair. They did far more than anybody else, working all day, and they got no more and no less than the workers who'd toiled for only an hour. The landowner, who surely would not have been surprised, tells one of them, maybe the only one who stuck around long enough to hear the explanation, calling him, "Friend." Didn't he agree to work for the usual daily wage? You can imagine how furious the man is, ready to throw the money back into the boss's face.

"Take what belongs to you and go," the landowner says. He's the boss; he can do what he wishes. After all, he didn't go against his word. He asks the rhetorical question, "Am I not allowed to do what I choose to do with what belongs to me?" And then he digs into the emotional heart of it. "Or are you envious because I am generous?" He ends with one of those mystical statements I tend to put into Jesus's mouth. Yes, Jesus is telling the story, but the words come from the landowner's mouth. "The last will be first, and the first will be last."

The last will be first, and the first will be last.

This story isn't about economics—it's about grace. And grace, by nature, isn't fair. It's more than fair. It's generous, unearned, and often surprising.

The more I think "That's not fair," the more I realize there's something here for me, something I need to pay attention to. *Thank you, Jesus.* I identify totally with the hardworking fellow who did what he was told to do, dutifully, and then watched with outrage at how someone else got just as much as he did but worked less. I think of myself as Mr. Good Guy. I do all the right things. I would help out at the office as much as needed, and then some. I burn the midnight oil. I send out appropriate emails, respond to all the texts. I'm on top of any schedule, often cranking out stuff early. *Look at me. Aren't I great?*

But then isn't it because I had advantages that go way back? I was born into a fully functional family, with loving—and hardworking—parents. I could absorb their values without ever having to be taught. We lived in a prosperous town with good schools, thanks very much to the good fortune of my own parents' families. This was their home turf too. I graduated from high school, went on to college, had the luxury of exploring several careers before settling down in the one that I found so fulfilling. Did I ever see someone bumped ahead of me in line, someone I didn't think deserved it? Not that I can remember. However, did I ever acknowledge all those advantages that made my life possible, growing up in a safe home, worshipping in a dynamic church, enjoying a good marriage, raising good kids, watching them launch themselves in their own fulfilling careers, and call it luck? No, it felt richly deserved. I put in my hours and got paid back in kind.

Jesus's story calls me to reconsider. What if the Guy in the sky, the divine landowner, were handing out things differently? Think about the travail that mid-afternoon laborer might have been through—struggling through setback after setback—just to show up. What did the five o'clock guy have to put up with? Had he just managed, with God's help, to give up the addiction that had almost destroyed him? Was showing up at this last minute an act of faith or divine providence? Why am I the one so quick to say, "It's not fair"? Isn't his life better proof of that?

Chances are, if you're reading this, you're not one of those latecomers. Or if you are, you aren't oblivious to your good fortune. Comparisons are odious. Look for ways you can be last rather than first. Compassion just might come easier, and mercy is never taken for granted. Sometimes my assumptions need to be shaken up, as they are by a story like this one.

At church when we choristers have to butt in line to take communion before singing the communion hymn, I'll mutter to myself, "The first shall be last, and the last shall be first." Ha, take that.

REFLECTIONS FOR MODERN LIVING

- Who are the "latecomers" in your life whom you've judged harshly?
- When have you received more than you deserved—and how did it change you?
- What does grace look like in your world today?
- Are you willing to celebrate others' blessings, even when they come after yours?

8

DON'T LET MONEY RULE YOU

How easy it is to get wrapped up in concerns about finances. Whether first-century Israelites or present-day Americans, people have always worried about money. How we always want more. Why not? With a little more money, wouldn't there be less to worry about? And heck, wouldn't that mean I'd be able to give more to others, let alone pay off the balance on my credit card . . . and what about that mortgage?

I can't tell you how often money worries and anxieties creep into my morning meditative, contemplative, this-is-when-I'm-supposed-to-be-thinking-about-God time.

Jesus understands us and money, even if what he says seems like it would be impossible to follow. Really, Jesus? How can I give away everything to the poor if I have a family to raise and kids to put through college, let alone health insurance to pay for and retirement savings to add to so I won't be a burden on those kids when I'm an old dude?

Let's go to the story of the young rich man and the eye of the needle when Jesus said—he really said it—"It is easier for a camel to go through the eye of a needle than for someone

who is rich to enter the kingdom of God." Wouldn't it be nice to think, as some have proposed, that "the eye of a needle" refers to a gate in ancient Jerusalem that was only open at night when the larger gate was closed, and a camel would need to stoop to get through. Supposedly, it's just a phrase they used to describe that gate. I don't buy it; nor do most scholars. Jesus means every challenging word he says, as he urges us to look deeper into our souls to know who we are and who God means us to be.

The young man had, as the Bible tells us, "many possessions," and a certain spiritual longing, coupled with a self-righteous attitude for being such a good, soulful seeker. He's come to Jesus, the good rabbi—Teacher, as he calls Jesus—with the burning question, "What good deed must I do to have eternal life?"

When he uses that phrase "eternal life," don't go too quickly to think he wants to know how to get into heaven. Like I've said, eternal life is something that starts here on earth, the door to the kingdom of God that's open to all of us.

Per usual, Jesus doesn't rush forward with an easy answer—a list, say, of all the things one must do—but rather responds with a question himself. Ask Jesus a question and you get a question back. If only Jesus gave a quick formula, something we can do and cross off the list. Done, Jesus, done. Instead, he asks us to look deeper into ourselves, to know why we even pose the question.

"Why do you ask me about what is good?" Jesus asks the young man. "There is only one who is good." God is good. Just add one letter to "God," at least in the English language, and you get "good." The two are so closely aligned.

"If you wish to enter into life, keep the commandments," Jesus goes on to say. Note: He's lingering over what the young man called "eternal." It's life as far as Jesus is concerned.

(Apologies here in that you're not hearing from someone who is an expert in Hebrew, Greek, or Aramaic, as much as I love hearing from such knowledgeable souls.)

"Which ones?" the young man asks. It looks like he really does want to know the answer so that he'll be able to check off each box. *Yes, I do that, and I do that, and I do that.* For a moment it seems that Jesus is going to truly satisfy the man's self-approving self-appraisal.

"You shall not murder; you shall not commit adultery," Jesus says, giving a list of those commandments, "you shall not steal; you shall not bear false witness; honor your father and mother; also, you shall love your neighbor as yourself."

Ah, what a relief. This young man has done all that. "I have kept all these," he says with assurance. And yet there's something still missing, some part of him that yearns. He wants to be filled, inside and out. "What do I still lack?" he asks. You can sympathize with the guy. He seems so sure of himself . . . and yet not so completely sure. It couldn't be easy to live with such mystical uncertainty. That's probably what motivated him to come to Jesus in the first place, wanting both to be reassured, "You're good, you're doing the right thing, you're living the good life," and also to be given some new challenge, some way forward, something beyond checking all the boxes.

Then, in one of the loveliest lines in the Bible, we learn that Jesus looked at the young man and "loved him," as Jesus loves us. Jesus understands.

"If you wish to be perfect, go, sell your possessions, and give the money to the poor, and you will have treasure in heaven," Jesus says.

If you wish to be perfect. What a challenge that would be, but yes, he wants perfection. It's out there somewhere, isn't it? Jesus is here to tell us about perfection. *Go, sell your possessions, and give the money to the poor.*

Maybe if the word "sell" weren't there, you could just give what you have to the poor, your extra cash. After all, you know they could use it. They're wanting in ways that the comfortable ones like us—those with many possessions—can hardly conceive. But Jesus is asking for more, far more. He's urging some sort of sacrificial giving, a means of entering the world of the poor and understanding it from the inside. You might have to give up one thing, but you'll have something even greater, treasure in heaven. Wasn't that what the young man was asking for in the first place? Wasn't that all he wanted?

Jesus concludes with the invitation, "Then come, follow me."

"Yes, Jesus, I want to follow you," I think. But would I be willing to pay such a hefty price? I'm not about to sell all my possessions. Okay, maybe I could unload some of them. Or give them to charity, where at least I can get a tax deduction. Check that box off. Jesus has got to understand what it's like to live in this modern era. We need to be cautious and responsible adults. I don't want to end up homeless and out on the street. But then, what do I really want? The question that begs a question.

Something interesting happens in the biblical story here. The young man doesn't continue the conversation. He gives up on the inner yearning that drew him to Jesus in the first place. He doesn't ask for more. Instead, he simply walks away, grieving, because as he knows better than anyone else, he has a lot—lots of possessions—and he's let them define who he is.

I want to scream out to him: "Wait. Don't leave. Stay there. Sit under a tree and listen to Jesus. Keep the dialogue going. You came to ask a question from the One who asks us even deeper questions. Ask again and again and again. Listen to the Lord's questions. The answer is not going to be about checking the boxes. It's going to be something even more profound.

Find out how you can give yourself away. Give it all up. Come up with a self-identity that isn't what you've been telling yourself. It has nothing to do with your possessions or your self-advertised decency and moral centeredness, all that so-called goodness that makes you so proud. Jesus is asking you to live on the edge. Give up, and you'll get something greater."

I remember pondering this story once as I was sitting on the subway train on my commute home from work, one of my daily avenues for pondering. I saw how often I was tempted to define myself by my possessions, the pictures on my phone, the job that gave me pleasure, the family that filled me with joy, the books on my shelf, the books I had written, the phone itself—how could I live without it? But what if I didn't think of those things as mine? Had I really earned them all? Wasn't I sometimes guilty of the same self-proclaimed holiness as the young man? I closed my eyes and prayed, "Have at it, Jesus. Have what I have as you wish and need. Let me never be possessed by what I own. I hardly own it anyway."

It's a prayer I try to say every day.

And hear what Jesus told the disciples after the rich young man left: "Truly I tell you it is easier for a camel to go through the eye of a needle than for someone who is rich to enter the kingdom of God."

That answer can be as unnerving for us as it was for the disciples. "Then who can be saved?" they asked. Was there no hope for anyone? Couldn't the least of us be excused for wanting to have what we had, and wanting what Jesus offers at the same time?

Jesus looked at them as he looks at us, with compassion. "For mortals it is impossible," he said. Our possessions will never preserve us from our mortality. Our faith will take us some place much, much higher. "But for God," as he says, "all things are possible." That's the way to live. That is true wealth.

For God, and with God, *all* things are possible. It's so easy to trust in the power of money; everything in our culture tells us so. Jesus is saying something different. It's even inscribed on our money. In God we trust. Not in the latest list of billionaires. In God we trust.

REFLECTIONS FOR MODERN LIVING

- What do you cling to that might be keeping you from spiritual freedom?
- When have you defined yourself by what you own—or what you lack?
- How might generosity be less about money and more about identity?
- Can you pray, even once this week, "Let me not be possessed by what I own"?

9

GENEROSITY IS ITS OWN REWARD

The people had been there for a long while. They'd come to listen to Jesus speak. No doubt, they'd come because they yearned for a miracle in their own lives too. Poor, hungry, adrift, their land dominated by an empirical foreign presence and power, they wanted words that would change things, heal things, knock things over. Truth to be told, they yearned for more than words. They wanted some power of their own. They'd waited so long, and nothing was getting better. Things only got worse for all the good people they knew. Where was God? Where was love? Where was compassion?

You've started a new TV show because everybody else says it's great. That you should just stick with it and see. You'll get it. You've heard about someone who was changed beyond words. Lucky him. Lucky her. Lucky them. Why couldn't it be you?

Time keeps rolling on. You listen and watch because that's what you're there for. You're with friends, family. You don't want to be the one who gives up early, but despite all that you've seen, all those words you've heard have meant nothing to you.

"Prove it," you say to yourself because you're too scared to say it aloud. If only you could be understood. If only someone knew who you really were, what you were really thinking, what *you* really had to say.

Why would they bother though? Why would they even care? Aren't they just as self-involved and selfish as you are at your worst private moments? Good thing nobody can read your mind and see the thoughts careening through your brain. Good thing you can't see theirs and know for sure what little they think of you, how little they think of you. One in a million? One in a thousand? You couldn't find yourself more alone than here, lost in a hungry, lonely crowd of four thousand, five thousand, the estimates beyond imagining.

Now you picture yourself in that biblical scene and for a moment, a fleeting moment, when you thought for sure that he knew you, that guy up there with all the words, with the stories that had you transfixed despite yourself, that had everybody listening, enchanted, together, everybody as one. But how could he possibly have seen that far, back to you, in the distance, talking directly to you? Was there another part of yourself that he noticed, some part that wanted to share and love and help the grizzled guy next to you who probably hadn't eaten in days—if you could only share with him, some tidbit or two to satisfy his hunger and thirst? Your hunger and thirst; it was yours too.

Words weren't going to do that. You'd spent enough of your born days swallowing your words. You knew how dangerous it was to speak out. You knew how impossible it was to challenge authority. No good came of it. Hide under a rock. Hide under a shadow. Disappear in the night air. Look out for number one. If you wouldn't, no one else would do it for you.

There were too many people though, all crammed in together because they wanted to hear for themselves, see for themselves, one of those miracles that was supposed to come from this human soul. Night was around the corner. Soon it would be time to trudge on back home. Get a bit of bread, a sliver of fish, a sip of water or wine without being noticed, because if you were noticed you would be expected to share.

Those who followed him, who stuck close to him, fishermen, laborers, surrounding him, the front guard, the rear guard, weren't they getting hungry too? No doubt they would pull him away so he could eat, and they could eat, far away from the crowd so they wouldn't have to share. Overstay your welcome? That would be easy enough to do here. Be gone. Disappear down the hill or step into one of those boats pulled up along shore and leave. Good riddance.

Good? If only there'd been more tangible good. It could be there, but you resist it because goodness itself is too dangerous. It will ask far more of you than you could possibly give back. Stay silent, you tell yourself. Stay asleep. Stay alone. Stay unheard.

He's turning his back on the crowd now, not even waiting for any questions or a smattering of applause, giving up on the healing. No miracle for these thousands who have waited so patiently, who so deserve it. It looks like he's gesturing—to a basket of loaves, to a paltry catch of fish, not even enough for the close followers at his left and right hands. They'd do their best to take it and run. Have at it before anyone else could take it, snatch it right out of their hands.

But what? Something else is happening. He's turning back to the crowd. That food, those loaves and fishes, they're evidently meant for all these people, all these hungry lost souls, hungry like you, thousands of them.

The sharing begins. Loaves and fishes and more fishes and loaves. Where did they come from? How could there be so many of them? The wave of food moves your way, like the tide coming in, reaching your outstretched hands until you're embarrassed that you've been caught begging for just a morsel of bread when, however it's happened—did people just start sharing what they had too?—a whole loaf lands in your hands, enough to split off and share with that guy who looks even hungrier than you.

People are leaving now, but they're leaving filled. You want to thank somebody, those followers perhaps, for giving like this, giving that's multiplied beyond all measure. Thank you, kind sir, thank you, my friend, thank you to the man who gives far more than words, as you wipe your mouth with satisfaction and sure, go ahead, take one of those salted fish. Bite on it and chew it, like you could bite and chew on his words.

People are collecting the leftover bits—leftovers, how in the world can there possibly be anything left over? Baskets and baskets of bones and dried crusts of bread accrue, more than there had ever been at the beginning.

"Give, and it will be given to you," Jesus said, but he didn't just say that—you could shrug it off if it were just words. These people weren't just eating words; they were feasting on food. You could feel it in your stomach, richly satisfying, unending delight.

Was this the miracle the crowd was expecting? No one could have expected this. Filled with Jesus's words, he took half the loaf he'd hidden under his robe and looked for someone he could share it with. Why take it home? It was all part of this feast, this feast of generosity and love.

Reflections for Modern Living

- Do you hesitate when asked to give?
- Do you ever see how something small—a few loaves and fishes—can grow exponentially when given away?
- When you look for increase in your life, is it about material things or spiritual ones?
- Have you ever found that miracles happened most in community?

10

DON'T BE DEFINED BY GROUP IDENTITY

Why does Jesus say such outrageous things? What kind of popularity contest is he so intent on losing?

"Whoever comes to me and does not hate father and mother, wife and children, brothers and sisters, yes, and even life itself, cannot be my disciple," he says.

Hate? *Really?* Did he actually say that? Aren't those the very people we're meant to love? Aren't they the ones who sacrificed for us, nurtured us, shaped us in their image? They loved us first. If we were to worship anyone, wouldn't they be first in line? But then—didn't we have to leave them in order to become ourselves?

We say family comes first. You work those long hours "for your family." To pay for school, to cover bills, to save for their future. That framed photo on your desk tells the world who you're doing it all for. Maybe the holiday card you mailed out tells the same story—everyone smiling, the kids squirming in your lap. You hold on tightly. But don't they have to let go to grow? Don't you?

It's easy to define yourself by family, just as you were once defined by your parents. Ask someone "Where are you

from?" and often, the answer goes back to their hometown—not where they live now, but where they first belonged. That place shaped you. So did the people who paid the down payment on your first car or helped you through school. Even the name you carry was handed to you. It all ties you to them—your family identity.

You may have said "I hate you" once in a moment of pain. Or whispered it to yourself. And yet, they didn't stop loving you. They knew—it was a phase. Maybe even a necessary one. Could it be that we must name what we "hate" in order to grow up? That we must detach to return in love? That only by seeing what we are not do we begin to see who we really are?

You wouldn't have known what home meant until you left it. You wouldn't have seen your blessings clearly until you realized not everyone had them. If you'd clung too closely, you would never have become the person God is calling you to be.

And when you grew and chose a partner, the pattern shifted—but repeated. You became "two." Decisions were no longer yours alone. And when that partner questioned you—your instincts, your beliefs—you were forced to admit you didn't know everything.

That's where the discomfort comes in. Being challenged feels like a threat. You resist it. You'd rather blame. Easier to hate the other than confront your own blind spots. But then, love steps in—love that requires forgiveness. Even of yourself.

And then, a child. That fragile little person breaks your heart wide open. You never knew love like this. You want to protect them forever. Until they say it. "I hate you." And you remember.

You remember what it means to break away in order to grow. To reject what once defined you in order to step into your own name, your own story, your own soul. That's what Jesus is getting at. One of the great dangers in life is being defined solely by where—or who—you came from. A group identity can become a shield, a shortcut, an illusion. You become "one of them"—your clan, your region, your party, your religion. But in doing so, you risk losing the very self God placed inside you.

Jesus knew how seductive that belonging could be. He knew how easily "us versus them" could creep in. And how, once you're inside that bubble, anything outside it becomes threatening. Even the truth. So he pushes us. Not to hate in the way we think of hate—but to loosen our grip on identity-as-inheritance. To see what we're holding onto too tightly. To let go of the small "us" so we can belong to something bigger: the kingdom of God.

When it all falls apart—your job, your health, your very identity—who will you reach for? You know Who. And that Who deserves a capital "W."

Only by losing the life you thought defined you can you find the one that truly does.

You wonder why Jesus would say such hard things. But if they hadn't challenged you, if they hadn't upset your assumptions, if they hadn't cracked open your comfort, they wouldn't have worked. Hate? Yes—hate the false attachments, the illusions, the small identities. Throw them away. Let them go.

Only then can you journey into love.

Reflections for Modern Living

- Have you ever clung too tightly to a group or identity that limited your growth?
- What might you need to release to become more fully yourself?
- Have you experienced transformation through detachment? What did it teach you?
- Where might God be calling you to loosen your grip and trust something deeper?

11

Do good. If necessary, let others know.

Jesus is a healer. Sometimes he seems glad to do it. Sometimes he seems hesitant. Sometimes he seems just exhausted. Indeed, what could be more tiring than being surrounded by needy souls who desperately seek a comforting, healing touch?

It's nice to think of Jesus as a healer. "Jesus, could you come and heal me?" we ask. Can you erase this depression that overwhelms me? Banish that pain that hits me unexpectedly? Reverse that scary diagnosis I just got? Take me out of my own fear of mortality?

We read about all the healings in Scripture and wonder how many of them could have been done through our own wonders of modern medicine. That man with some dreadful skin disease—could it not be treated by one of our fine dermatologists? The paralyzed man whose friends make a hole in the roof to lower him on a mat to reach Jesus's healing hands—might he not have been fixed up by one of those simple surgical procedures that are common, like a hip replacement? As for the blind, we have miraculous laser surgery, not to mention cochlear implants and hearing aids for the deaf or organ transplants for the suffering. Could whatever Jesus did be unnecessary today?

The stories of how he cured can seem bewildering. Take the woman who was hemorrhaging for a dozen years. She had seen every doctor she could find, spending all of her money, and her condition only worsened. But with Jesus all she needed to do was touch the hem of his garment from behind—without him seeing her—and the bleeding stopped. She was cured. Even with the crowd around him, Jesus felt the power sucked out of him. When he turned around and asked, "Who touched me?" she wanted to disappear. It would be entirely unacceptable in that time and culture for a woman like herself, especially one with a hemorrhage, to be seen touching another person, let alone the Lord. Couldn't it just be a secret? Finally, she identified herself, falling before him, trembling in fear.

"Your faith has made you well," he said. "Go in peace." That's all. He didn't even need to consciously touch her for it to happen. Her faith was good enough.

We fixate on the illness, trying to translate it into modern terms, as though we were some cosmic diagnosticians casting a backward glance with all our improved scientific knowledge and wisdom. Life expectancy has been wonderfully extended in our modern age—for most of us, at least—and we would have Jesus the healer around for those conditions that still can't be cured by our good doctors, that uncurable strain of cancer, say, or that drastic heart condition or lung disease.

But in all our narrowness of thinking, aren't we inclined to miss one of Jesus's main points? Wouldn't it have been kinder for him to ignore that woman he'd just cured and let her sneak off in quiet reassurance?

No, he wanted to make a point, something that I think is crucial to hold on to when we look at any of his healings. These were *healings*, not just cures.

Often enough, as with the woman suffering from the hemorrhage, his healings were something done in front of others. He wanted the people around to know. He wasn't just demonstrating some magical power to rid a woman of a persistent bleeding; he was trying to heal the crowd too. He was making a public show to rid them of their own prejudices and biases, which were as, if not more, dangerous than any illness out there.

Their thinking would have had to change, maybe that very minute. They would have to go from "What are you doing, Lord?" to "She is one of us, Lord, isn't she? She is good, lovable, loved by God." By having communion with the ceremonially "unclean," Jesus was showing everyone that they should too. Jesus isn't just healing the one, showing off God's power. He is trying to heal all of us. If we would only look. If we would only pay attention.

Like Job's accusers, his so-called friends, I am always quick to see a reason for anyone's illness or suffering. "She's put on a lot of weight," I'll say to myself. "No wonder she's out of breath all the time." "Look at all that terrible stuff he eats. Fried food. Heaping dishes of ice cream. I'll bet he's going to end up a diabetic." "Another glass of wine? Another cocktail? He'll be paying the price all too soon." See what's really there? The smug self-congratulation, the longing to make a comparison that proclaims, "God, at least I'm not like that."

But then, why do I suffer? Why do I have to make a trip to urgent care or haul myself into the ER? Why do I take all these pills? Why must I have that surgical procedure? Why do I not want to get out of bed this morning? What does that blood pressure monitor say?

Do I forget that I need to be healed too? Not just physically, but in my mind's eye? How I need to see the world through the Lord's loving, caring, forgiving eyes! To truly love my neighbor as myself should not come out of some judgmental act of comparison. If I can only feel good by lowering my appraisal of someone else, how good am I really?

The Pharisees got all twisted out of shape when Jesus healed on a Sabbath, a holy day when no work was supposed to be done, even the good work of healing. I suspect that what really upset them was seeing their views of good and bad turned upside down. The leper, the paralytic, the deaf, the blind, the bleeding, the crippled—clearly God didn't love those wounded souls as much as God loved the self-aggrandizing Pharisee, did he? *Did* he?

The healing wasn't meant just for the poor, suffering soul; it was also meant for those who watched and those who saw. This was an opportunity for them too.

Sometimes when Jesus heals, he tells the healed person not to talk about it. Don't go around showing off. Don't tell the world who cured you. Don't spread the word around about this healer. Is it possible that by doing so we'd focus on the cure rather than the healing? The healing was for the group; the cure was for that individual. If you weren't there, would you know that? Would you feel it, experience it? The danger could be that you'd be declaring, "Look, look at me," rather than "Look, look at you" and "Look, look at Jesus."

We are meant to do good, but doing good is not our report card.

REFLECTIONS FOR MODERN LIVING

- Do you ever give anonymously? Why?
- What does "doing good" mean to you?
- Can you make each day an opportunity to help others, even if no one sees it?
- How do you judge others? How can you love them instead?

12

HUMILITY IS EVERYTHING

Humility is hard to talk about because once you bring it up, acknowledging its importance and power, are you really being so humble? Can you talk about it and have it at the same time? In its truest form, humility doesn't even know itself. For a clearer picture of it, Jesus tells a story, as is his wont.

Two men go up to the temple to pray, one of them a Pharisee and one a tax collector. Those contrasting identities would have been very clear to his listeners. We can't imagine how awful tax collectors were for the Judean people. First off, they were generally turncoats, Jews who were working for the Roman occupiers, collaborators in the worst sense of the word. Instead of fighting the bad guys, they were working hand-in-glove with the enemy. And often enough, they cheated as they did it, putting something in their own well-stuffed pockets.

When they skimmed off the top, taking more than what was owed and putting it in their own pockets, who were they taking it from? Their very own people, fellow believers, fellow Jews. Their Roman bosses surely understood and knew, turning a blind eye to it.

No one likes paying taxes. Well, except for my dad. On April 15, as he worked feverishly to finish up the forms and

get them to the post office before midnight, he would tell me, "It's an honor to pay taxes." An honor, he said. "It's our way of helping our country and helping others." I wish that were my knee-jerk reaction. I'm more likely to become obsessed about all the deductions I can possibly find, adding them up. Doing good by paying taxes? Well, aren't I doing good by giving to charity . . . so that I can get a tax deduction for it?

Tax collectors were easy enemies, dupes for the taking. As is often the case, it's easiest to demonize someone who is like you and also not like you, perhaps because you're jealous of them. Why didn't you sign up to be a tax collector yourself and make a little extra on the side? It's easier just to hate the guys. The Roman rulers were off in their palaces, wining and dining, where you couldn't even see them, but tax collectors? They were around every corner—you couldn't avoid them. With all that money they earned plus what they skimmed off the top, they were well-fed, well-dressed, well-housed—inescapable adversaries.

You couldn't avoid the Pharisees either, scrupulous as they were in observing the Jewish law and showing it. They kept up with the traditional practices of the faith. They didn't eat without a ceremonial washing of their hands. They studied the Scriptures and upheld them, always looking for converts to their holy ways. They believed in the notion of resurrection and taught in the synagogue, passing along their insights and knowledge. They avoided being around "sinners," like those tax collectors, and separated themselves simply by rigorously observing their beliefs. Calling someone a Pharisee today is usually a negative; you're pointing out someone's holier-than-thou approach. But Pharisees weren't all bad; in fact, some of them saw the light and followed Jesus, as we'll see, without denigrating their spiritual practice. They became illustrative of how dangerous it can be (watch out, Rick) to think you're better than anyone else.

Ever put yourself on a pedestal like that?

So, back to Jesus's story, one of my favorites. As the two men went up to the temple to pray, the Pharisee stood by himself—stood out to himself—and prayed aloud, "God, I thank you that I am not like other people." And if you wondered, he spells it out. He's not like thieves, rogues, adulterers, or even that tax collector sullying up the temple steps. A good Pharisee, he fasts twice a week and gives a tenth of his income away, just what the Scriptures prescribe—a perfect tithe. He feels pretty good about himself, and that's the very problem, because if you're in a mood like that, proclaiming those prayers, are you really so prayerful? In such a state, how open are you going to be to what God might be saying to you?

In dramatic contrast, the tax collector, the publican, is standing far off, hoping not to be noticed. He doesn't even look up to heaven, the godly realm, but beats his breast, saying, praying, "God, be merciful to me, a sinner!"

Jesus calls out the latter, not the former. It's the tax collector who has it right and for a single simple, complex reason, as Jesus explains, "For all who exalt themselves will be humbled, but all who humble themselves will be exalted."

Why is that? Perhaps it's because when you're in that self-inflating mode of self-congratulation, you're not open to hearing larger truths. You're not in a place that allows for growth and transformation. You're not ready to learn new things—not just about others but also about yourself. Take it from one who knows. (Insert smiley face emoji, lest I be accused of false humility.)

The other place, the lowly position of the tax collector/publican, can be much harder. Feeling bereft, feeling lonely, feeling "less than" rather than "more than," suffering, wondering, seeing yourself as small not large, uncertain and unattractive, these are hard places to be. What's more, there's little in our larger world to make them seem appealing. Can you imagine going into a job interview and spelling out what your failings just might be—with all those laudable achievements listed on your resume? As I said before, when job candidates are asked to enumerate their weaknesses, the one they're most likely to claim is "impatience," in the not-so-secret knowledge that that one failing will make them look even more appealing. Isn't an impatient person more likely to get something done?

Humility. It is so tricky. Sometimes it can mean hearing and accepting those good things people might say about you or send in a text or email—to receive, truly receive, all those compliments. False humility is almost always painfully obvious. The challenge for me is aspiring to humility while still savoring the little (or not so little) inner voice that says, "Good job" and "Great work. Nicely done." Being a little pleased with myself can supply the energy to keep the mental treadmill running. I think of our grandson Silas, who when he was two years old would often offer the refrain "I did it." *I did it.* Once when we drove for three minutes to the pizza joint and the kid, who could get terribly carsick, made it without throwing up, he proclaimed from his car seat, "I did it." That, too, can be a source of humility. Especially when it's "I did it with God's help."

Where I step into the deepest humility, like that fellow beating his breast on the temple steps, is when I enter the spiritual life. As I sit on our lumpy sofa in the morning and indulge in my sacred quiet time, seeking God in prayer, all sorts of ungodly thoughts will enter the terrain, like the stuff on my Google calendar, the emails I haven't responded to, the text messages in my phone, a recent charge on my credit card. When I circle back to the divine, I'm filled with true humility. *Good Lord, have mercy on me, a sinner.*

Sin is real. My failings are something I don't ever want to lose sight of. If I don't know what I'm doing wrong, how will

I ever get things right? It's not always easy. I've been known to offend people just by indulging in a bad joke. One of the gifts of the workplace, and one of the aids we can give each other in spiritual community, is to see how we're failing and confront it. Turn it into an opportunity that will allow us to grow. Humility is an avenue to happiness, true happiness. And when it really happens it's out of my hands. It comes in the heavenly passive voice: *all who humble themselves will be exalted.* Amen.

REFLECTIONS FOR MODERN LIVING

- What do you feel most humble about?
- Do you secretly compare yourself to others, whether favorably or unfavorably?
- Have you ever seen how a humbling spiritual experience can be a source of growth?
- What does it mean to you to humble yourself before the Lord?

13

Worry Not

Don't worry? That's hard—so hard that it's both a relief and worrisome to hear it from Jesus. He knows about worry, how very human it is, how necessary it can sometimes feel, how we sometimes make it a motivating force. What would we do without it?

My wife has something she calls "prophylactic worry." She'll look for things to worry about in advance so that they don't happen. After all, it's the things we *don't* worry about that can take us by surprise. If you bring your umbrella with you, say, you're less likely to be caught in a downpour. Or if you consider the worst possible scenario before you go to the doctor's office, you'll be relieved by the mild diagnosis. Check through the list of worries, consider them one by one, let your imagination expand on all the various possibilities—doesn't that somehow save us from the worst thing that could happen? We've already fantasized about it. It's there in our head. Won't we be better able to handle whatever comes our way?

What on earth is Jesus telling us? What are we supposed to do if not worry?

"Think of something else," he says. Consider the flowers of the field and how they grow. Look up to the birds of the air and how they provide for themselves. They flap their wings and then catch the updraft of air that sends them soaring, floating to their destination. When they land on the ground, they spend plenty of time picking at what will feed them. The raptors look like they're spotting the possibilities, scoping them out from their heavenly vantage point. And nature, the Creator, has endowed them with the wisdom to fly to more temperate, hospitable climes when the cold weather comes. God takes care of them. They don't need to worry.

"Can any of you by worrying add a single hour to your span of life?" Jesus asks.

Don't you feel like saying, *Well, yes, Jesus, I think I can.* Didn't it take some worrying for you to make that dreaded appointment with a financial planner or listen to some more knowledgeable friend to learn about what to do with that 401(k) to get ready for retirement (as if you could ever truly be ready)? Wasn't it worry that motivated you to schedule that doctor's appointment in the first place, or that dental visit? If you hadn't worried a bit, would you have bought those vitamins that are supposed to be good for your health? Isn't it worry that makes you better at your job, the way you can anticipate some of the challenges coming up and be all too ready to meet them?

Yes and no. There's something a little dangerous here. We might just be a little too in love with our powers of worry, developing them far beyond what is necessary. We might, in fact, confuse worry with work.

Let's look at those flowers growing in the field. Their roots dig deep into the soil, pulling up the nutrients, feeding and drinking what nature provides. Their leaves capture the sunlight, little factories of photosynthesis, turning the carbon dioxide into oxygen and energy. Seemingly effortlessly, they can produce food that we eat, flowers turning into fruit, eventually reproducing themselves in the seeds that fall into the soil and spring up with new flowers. "They neither toil nor spin," as Jesus says, "yet I tell you, even Solomon in all his glory was not clothed like one of these."

Seems to me that Jesus isn't just giving us a sermon here but offering a means to an end. Worry got you all tangled up? Is anxiety freezing you from being able to move forward or make any sort of creative progress? Look out the window. Go outside. Gaze up. Look down. Take in the beauty of the world. Smell it, taste it, hear it, savor it. Check out the little blossom you plopped into a vase and set on your kitchen counter. Run your hands through the feather you picked off the ground on a hike. Smile at the photo of a blooming poppy or a flight of migrating geese that you clipped from a magazine years ago and posted on your refrigerator or saved on your phone. Was it worry that made you do it? Wasn't it delight instead?

Our brains are constructed so that we naturally think ahead. I pull up Google Calendar to see what I'm supposed to do tomorrow and next week and next month or to try to remember what I did last month. I look at my weather app to see if it's going to rain or not (instead of just looking out the window). I scroll through some spreadsheet in my head. But do I need to wallow in the worries that might accompany any such exercise? Need it be anxiety that prompts me?

Years ago, I remember interviewing a wise therapist who described that feature of our brains. The anxiety can propel us forward if we keep it behind us, she said, like the propeller of a motorboat. It's hardly worry at all. However, if we put it in front, it can wrap around our necks, choking us. The choice is ours.

We want to use worry to ensure our safety and security, to have that roof over our head and that next meal in the refrigerator, as well as the money in the bank to pay the bills. Jesus asks us to go back and reconsider the grass in the field, here today and then thrown into the fire tomorrow. If God clothes the natural world with such splendor, wouldn't he do the same for us—and then some? Jesus knows how we worry constantly, asking ourselves "What shall we eat?," "What shall we drink?," "What shall we wear?," or it might be "How shall I respond to that text that's driving me nuts?" or "How is my kid going to do on that test tomorrow?" or "Will their team lose again on Saturday?" Worries, worries, worries.

God knows how our minds work and overwork. We want to prove how clever we are. We want to anticipate everything. We want to show that we're ahead of the game. And we allow ourselves to get smaller instead of bigger. Jesus offers a solution, something for our overthinking minds, something to concentrate on. Pick the big thing, not the niggling little thing.

"But seek first the kingdom of God and his righteousness," Jesus says, "and all these things will be given to you as well." My head goes into song, a tune we sang in Sunday school. "Seek ye first the kingdom of God, and his righteousness . . ." There is a reason those words stick in my craw with a tune that's inescapable. "So do not worry about tomorrow, for tomorrow will bring worries of its own. Today's trouble is enough for today." *Today's trouble is enough for today.* Ain't it the truth!

Has indulging in a panoply of worries ever really made for a better day? Isn't there that downside—one that Jesus understands—that the worries only take away from the goodness of life? They add stress to our days, and stress can be a major cause of illness, depression, unhappiness, despair. Let me go for something bigger. The recipe is right there. *Seek ye first God's kingdom and righteousness.* I promise to hold that in my head, the bigger picture, something sublime and mind-bending. It's part of my prayer practice every day. *Rick, what's on your mind?* A world transformed by God's love. I need it, we need it. Be present in the day, this day, today.

REFLECTIONS FOR MODERN LIVING

- What are your deepest worries?
- How can you let love drive you forward rather than letting fear hold you back?
- Can you structure your day so that the goodness of God doesn't get overpowered by the worrisome headlines?
- How can reflecting on nature—the birds, the flowers, the trees, the breeze—help you with your worries?

14

Evil exists. And it knows when it is threatened.

Often in Scripture, it's the good guys who take a while to recognize Jesus's divinity and power. This is not the case with the evil forces in the world. They know right away when there's a threat to their livelihood and existence. They see it coming.

In the first chapter of the Gospel of Mark, Jesus is teaching in the synagogue, captivating his listeners with his knowledge and authority, when there appears in their midst a man with "an unclean spirit." "What have you to do with us, Jesus of Nazareth?" the spirit spouts off with a vengeance. "Have you come to destroy us? I know who you are, the Holy One of God." Like some character in a scary movie, the man is possessed by a demon. Evil has taken him over.

At first, I want to say that such a thing wouldn't really happen today. I like to think that people are good. They might be misled, but they're basically good. "Misled" is the key word. (For a long time as a kid when I read that word "misled," I called it "mizzled" in my head. I knew two words: "misled" that people said and "mizzled" that I read. Talk about being misled!) But there are forces out there luring us down the wrong

path, dressed in all sorts of garb, appealing to our darker sides: gluttony, lasciviousness, hatred, envy, wrath, greed, pride, idolatry, sloth. I can tell myself that we don't worship idols like golden calves, then I log onto social media or scroll through the news and see the glossy images of fame and fortune capturing my attention, feeding my envy. Idolatry might be one of our worst faults because we're so ignorant of it. We don't even see it in ourselves.

What then happens to that man tortured by the unclean spirit? In an instant Jesus rebukes the spirit. "Be silent and come out of him," he says. And the unclean spirit convulsing the man and "crying with a loud voice, came out of him." It's not such a pretty picture. Evil doesn't want to let go so fast. No wonder it felt so threatened.

It's not always fun or easy to acknowledge our dark sides. We see it in our families and friends, even in places as good and holy as our worship communities. Think about your church or maybe your twelve-step group. True confession: I'm not nearly the good, kindly, polite gentleman I try to look like. If you could read my mind, it wouldn't always be a pretty picture. Not for nothing do I need to beg for forgiveness.

Know yourself, the good and the bad. Jesus can't rectify any of it until you admit your faults, opening yourself up to change. The ritual of confession, silent or aloud, shared or private, is invaluable. Evil knows this, like that demon that knew who Jesus was, its existence on the line.

Later in the book of Mark, Jesus's adversaries proposed that he was using his own demonic power to cast out the demons (clever, evil, clever). Jesus responded, "How can Satan cast out Satan?" And then in one of his most quotable lines, referenced by Abraham Lincoln in his legendary "house divided" speech about a government that was half-slave and half-free, he says: "If a kingdom is divided against itself, that kingdom cannot stand. And if a house is divided against itself, that house will not be able to stand." Jesus is here on earth to do business with Satan, and he is showing us how. "If Satan has risen up against himself and is divided," he goes on to say, "he cannot stand, but his end has come."

This language can make us uncomfortable. We'd rather that the idea of wrestling with Satan be saved for a creepy sci-fi film, not something we need to handle on earth. And yet, and yet . . . I see a lot of hatred and strife in our world, the means used to justify the end, all the worse when it's clothed in self-righteousness (you notice how I keep coming back to that—it's one of my worst sins, despite my posture as Mister Good Guy). "I hate that dude because he's wrong, and I'm going to prove it." Wait—didn't Jesus tell us to love our enemies?

In another story recounted in Matthew, Mark, and Luke—the so-called synoptic Gospels—Jesus heals a man with an unclean spirit who lived among the tombs. It was impossible to stop the poor man, even with chains and shackles. "The chains he wrenched apart," as Mark puts it, "and the shackles he broke in pieces." No one was strong enough to restrain him. Night and day he lurked among the tombs, howling and bruising himself with stones. "When he saw Jesus from a distance, he ran and bowed down before him, and he shouted at the top of his voice, 'What have you to do with me, Jesus, Son of the Most High God?'" He knew Whom he was talking to, even when others didn't quite trust in that godly identity.

Jesus spoke back to the unclean spirit and asked his name. He, or rather they—a plural they—replied famously, "My name is Legion, for we are many."

There happened to be a herd of swine feeding on a nearby hill, and the unclean spirits begged Jesus, "Send us into the swine; let us enter them." Now the story becomes a little more complicated for the modern reader because we like to believe

Jesus loved animals—he did indeed. But then think about pigs back in Judea—wholly unkosher, something the Judeans couldn't eat. Hence, these swine were probably not raised by Jesus's own people, or certainly not for them to eat, but more likely for the Roman occupiers. Some say that the swine are symbolic of the Roman forces. Note the request doesn't come from the tormented man but from the unclean spirits themselves.

Jesus obliged, and the unclean spirits—named Legion (like the Roman Legion)—entered the herd, about two thousand pigs, and the animals rushed down the steep bank to the sea, all of them drowned.

What an impressive healing, vivid, shocking, and outrageous. But what does it mean? The idea that someone can be possessed feels so wrong. And yet, when I note someone on the New York subway, struggling with mental illness, shouting, flailing, many of them suffering from the consequences of drug addiction, they seem attacked inside by legions. I wish I had the power like Jesus to heal them in one fell swoop. When someone asks for money, I try to have a buck or two on hand to give away—with prayers that it will serve some good. The response, like I said, is almost always "God bless you." I don't think it's just manipulation—how many of their givers are God people? Somehow, they want to see God at work and give it a name. Like those souls who recognized Jesus for who he was.

Evil cannot always be so quickly excised and put to rest. Let me quote a long passage from Matthew: "When the unclean spirit has gone out of a person, it wanders through waterless regions looking for a resting place, but it finds none. Then it says, 'I will return to my house from which I came.' When it comes, it finds it empty, swept, and put in order. Then it goes and brings along seven other spirits more evil than itself, and they enter and live there; and the last state of that person is worse than the first. So it will be also with this evil generation."

Watch out. Evil can generate more evil. It's out there—and in here. Don't put a smug face on it. Confront it, acknowledge it, call out to Jesus. After all, it often knows who Jesus is.

REFLECTIONS FOR MODERN LIVING

- What do you think Jesus would define as evil in our modern world?
- Can you respond to evil as Jesus would, with transforming love and compassion?
- What would you describe as idolatry in today's everyday life, and can you address it in your life?
- Can you be specific as you pray "Deliver us from evil," the prayer Jesus gave us?

15

WELCOME YOUR INNER CHILD

We were all children once. We grew up. We became responsible adults. We gave up our childish ways. We launched ourselves in careers. We took on roles to show that we were serious, committed, trustworthy, demanding, and impatient too. Any boss could give us a task, no matter how niggling, and we would get it done. Naturally we expected rewards for our behavior, a paycheck, a salary, a bonus, a promotion. That's what grown-ups got, models of authority.

And yet there was always the danger that we would lose sight of something we had as children: innocence, curiosity, playfulness, imagination, trust, humility, enthusiasm, love—the list could go on and on. Maybe you were sent off to Sunday school, as I was, where you would find a picture of Jesus surrounded by children, the smallest one sitting in his lap. Warm and inviting images, they were surely meant to say, "See, Jesus cares about *you*. Jesus cares about the little ones."

Don't we need that warm fuzziness in our lives? It's good to be reminded at any age that Jesus cares about us. We listened in church to the story from the Bible. Parents were bringing

their children to Jesus—like our parents—so he might pray for them, protect them from the evils of the world, heal them from any suffering. The disciples, worried about protecting Jesus—and mirroring the biases of their era—tried to put a halt to it. After all, wasn't Jesus a big shot? Why should he waste time with these little kids? He had more important things to do with his time, more important souls to reach.

Jesus stopped them. "Let the little children come to me," he said, "and do not stop them; for it is to such as these that the kingdom of heaven belongs." Pause and paint a picture of it: Jesus smiling, the kids clambering over and around him, with delight and awe. *Such as these*, they are meant to be models, models for us.

It's easy to lose track of what a revolutionary Jesus was. Children did not have much status in the first-century Judean world. They were expected to work for the family as soon as possible, to do as told, to help take care of the animals, do their share of household chores, and help with the cooking, cleaning, serving. Children were biddable but not independent beings, low on the totem pole.

Jesus, however, elevates them, not just for their own sakes but to teach a lesson to those adults—the disciples here—listening in. "Thanks, guys, for trying to protect me," Jesus might have said or thought. "Yes, I am a busy man with a full plate, but these little ones count for a lot too." *Let them come to me.* More than that, he's giving us a lesson. *For it is to such as these that the kingdom of heaven belongs.*

What is it that children have? What inborn qualities are they given that can open the kingdom of God to them? It should be as obvious to us as it would have been to Jesus's listeners—and even more shocking to them. Yes, take on the responsibilities of parenthood and be a reliable contributor to society's needs in the workplace and at home, but not at the expense of closing yourself off to those God-given traits that can give us joy—like I said, curiosity, playfulness, imagination, creativity, trust, humility, enthusiasm, love.

We often accompany our grandchildren to church—after all, their dad is a minister. At the nine o'clock service, specifically geared to young ones and families, there are coloring books, crayons, craft projects, collages, storytelling, and music to dance to and sing to. As always, there is a sermon, and as I've seen, the children are encouraged to participate in it.

Not long ago, the preacher was retelling the story of St. Martin, who cut his cloak in half to share with a beggar shivering from the cold. The speaker invited the kids to help act out the story, offering up a plastic sword. I watched in wonder as our then-two-and-a-half-year-old grandson stepped forward—no doubt attracted by the sword—and was drafted to play the role of the beggar.

Will he remember this when he's grown up? Probably not. But I won't forget it. What I hope stays with him forever is that crayons and coloring paper and imagination and playacting—touching base with those parts of yourself—are part of what God wants for us. We are never to lose sight of that. In my adulthood it has been easy to overlook those parts of myself. After all, what were they paying me for at work? What would my colleagues have thought if I'd brought some crayons to that important year-end meeting in the conference room—gazing at the PowerPoint riddled with statistics and numbers? They might have rolled their eyes and thought, "There goes Rick, tumbling off the deep end."

These two parts of our being can coexist. The innocent, childlike wonder can make friends with the number-crunching cognitive awareness. You don't have to take the crayons or markers to the conference room meeting. You can hold them in your imaginative head, coloring your understanding, and be a better colleague and/or boss, spouse or parent, too, because of it. When you do that mandated year-end review of a colleague or an underling—or you are that colleague or underling—you have the added compassion and insights into what they're going through. Your inner child is your friend.

What is obviously significant to Jesus's teaching about welcoming the child is the absolute trust that children have, their unconscious willingness to look up to adults. It should never be abused. We've already touched on this, but humility in children is especially significant because a child is so ignorant of it. Bragging about being humble is a self-defeating prospect. A child just is. What I treasure about my childhood is being able to go to Mom or Dad with a story, a picture, a puppet I'd made, a song I wanted to sing. I knew I had a captive audience, someone who would nod, smile, give me a hug. How could I not believe in God's ever-present love?

The tragedy in our society—this must break Jesus's heart—is the countless incidents where a child's trust is severely hampered, where the adults who are in charge wreak havoc with a child's natural innocence and need for love, rejection and abandonment becoming burdens of a lifetime. The trauma of such a childhood is something Jesus understands only too well, one more reason the children need to come to him—as does the wounded adult child in us—for his healing touch.

What is it that a child has? "Who is the greatest in the kingdom of heaven?" the disciples asked him in another incident—hoping to stump him, perhaps, as much as they longed for an answer. Whatever it might have been, the answer could not have been what they were expecting. It wouldn't have been enough for Jesus just to tell them in words. Like the vivid witness he is for God's love, he *shows* them. He calls a child whom he puts among them and then says, "Truly I tell you, unless you change and become like children, you will never enter the kingdom of heaven."

Unless you change. Do something different. Change your thinking and behavior. Look deep within.

"Whoever becomes humble like this child is the greatest in the kingdom of heaven. Whoever welcomes one such child in my name welcomes me," he says. That childlike willingness to trust is everything. It kicks over the normal pecking order, reversing the lineup. The first shall be last, and the last shall be first. Keep hold of that inner child.

Reflections for Modern Living

- What does your inner child take especial delight in?
- Can you remember and reconstruct some of the key moments of your childhood?
- What makes you smile and laugh like a child? Where can you be curious like a kid?
- Do you have any trauma associated with childhood? If so, can you invite Jesus into your life and that child's life for healing?

16

Jesus Heals Both Body and Soul

We live in an age of sophisticated, scientifically proven medical care. When you're sick, you consult a doctor. You take medicine that has been tested and shown to work. You might have to go to the hospital for surgery—or a procedure, as they might call it. There are countless tests to determine just what's wrong and what should be treated. You put yourself in a state of deep trust, trusting the tests, the doctors, the treatments. You find yourself in a situation where you must put hope into a medical system. Your body needs help. These good caregivers are doing their best to respond to those needs.

I'm not arguing with any of that or with the care and concern of doctors, medicine, nurses, hospital staff. I have been helped by all of the above. I would not be sitting here typing on my computer without such care. But sometimes our medical system has trouble acknowledging how the spirit and soul need healing too. *Soul? What's that?* And where actually is it? Can it be found on an X-ray or an MRI? Will it turn up in a blood test? Modern medicine can do miraculous heart and lung and kidney and liver transplants; no one has ever asked it to transplant a soul.

In our communities of faith, we have means and ways of praying for others. There are prayer lists, emails that go out among the community, urgent requests, news that must be shared, sometimes publicly, sometimes anonymously. "Please pray for . . ." Fill in the blank with name and need. Or if it feels just a little too private for that, silently offer up the name, knowing that God knows what the need is. Quite frankly, I always find it easier to say a prayer with more information, not less. I like to be able to picture the prayer recipient in their bed with that hacking cough or the broken limb or the paraphernalia of an operation. A question, though: Do I pray for their souls? Do I ask God that their sins be forgiven? Is it even fair to link their sins to their fragile physical state? That doesn't seem so nice.

Why, then, does Jesus seem to do so?

Let's go to one of my favorite healing stories in the Bible, one I've briefly mentioned, the healing of a paralytic who is lowered through the roof to reach Jesus.

Jesus is inside a house—the Gospel accounts differ as to exactly where—preaching and teaching and presumably healing. Some friends have brought their paralyzed friend to be healed by Jesus. There is such a crowd they can't even get in through the front door. They can't get Jesus's attention from there, so they do something that seems a little bizarre to us. They take their paralytic friend up to the flat roof, probably only a walk up one flight, and dig through the clay and sticks to make a hole above Jesus, lowering their friend down. They might have been carrying him on a make-shift stretcher, easy enough to help the paralyzed man down with their arms and hands. Or maybe they tied a rope to it or lowered him on a sheet. All that effort makes them a key part of the story.

Where does healing come from? From our prayer communities, from our concerned loved ones, from those who care about us and are willing to do whatever it takes. "What a friend we have in Jesus" goes the old song. What a friend we have in our friends who bring us to Jesus. Jesus sees their faith. It must have moved him. Right away, he says to the paralytic, "Your sins are forgiven."

What are the man's sins, and how does Jesus even know of them? And how did the man react? Did he say, "Jesus, these guys brought me here to be healed of my paralysis so that I might walk someday . . . and what? You're telling me my sins are forgiven?" Does this mean that the only reason we get sick and suffer physically is because God is punishing us for some sins we might be committing? As a friend of mine used to say, with exasperation, "That's a fine way for God to behave!"

I don't think that's Jesus's point. Elsewhere, this is in the Gospel of John, we read a story of Jesus spotting a man who had been blind since birth and his disciples asked him, "Rabbi," which means "teacher"—as he is their teacher—"who sinned? This man or his parents, that he was born blind?" There is that urge in humanity to blame a disability on someone or something. It's got to be someone's fault rather than blind fate. There is no such thing as blind fate in God's world. Everything matters. "Neither this man nor his parents sinned," Jesus says. "He was born blind so that God's works might be revealed in him." He is there for the miracle that Jesus will perform.

Let's go back to the paralytic whose sins are forgiven. He still hasn't gotten up and walked yet. Wait . . . isn't that what his friends brought him there for?

Jesus is not just a doctor—and teacher—for the body, ready to give lectures to a roomful of med students. He has a much bigger message, something we can forget in our airtight, well-roofed homes as well as the hospitals that help us. I think of words inscribed in stone in the original building of NewYork-Presbyterian Hospital, the medical center where my doctors all work and the place where I have had surgery and excellent care. The sign is over a side door, easy enough to ignore, and dates from an early era. "From the Most High cometh healing," it says, engraved in stone, a biblical reference (though a doctor buddy of mine said was it was often quoted when he and his buddies, fellow med students, partied—ha).

Your sins are forgiven. Those dark, self-blaming, angry, hateful sides of your nature, those places where you can do inner torture even without any accompanying illness, those places where you deny any existence of God, not only in the beyond but in yourself, they can be at the root of incalculable misery. Jesus is here to heal our souls.

As well as our bodies.

In this instance with the paralytic, Jesus wants to make an important point to his listeners, especially the scribes and Pharisees who have gotten the rudiments of faith backward, focusing on strict observance of the law, at the risk of ignoring the powerful ways God brings love to all of us. They think they have now caught this teacher—this so-called teacher—proclaiming something blasphemous. After all, no one can forgive sins but God and God alone.

They are right. And they are also hopelessly wrong because they refuse to believe, and can't recognize, *Who* is doing the talking and *Who* is performing these miracles. Jesus will tell them and show them, as he does often enough. He knows what they're saying to themselves—Jesus always knows what's going on in our heads—and challenges their thinking. "Why do you raise such questions in your hearts?" he asks. "Which is easier, to say to the paralytic, 'Your sins are forgiven,' or to say, 'Stand up and take your mat and walk'?" What is it that we want to hear Jesus say to us? How can we be helped the most?

"But so that you may know that the Son of Man has authority on earth to forgive sins," he goes on, addressing the paralytic directly, "I say to you, stand up, take your mat, and go to your home." The paralyzed man stood up and immediately took the mat and went out of the house in front of everybody. The crowd was amazed and in awe. They saw that it was God in action, exclaiming, "We have never seen anything like this."

They have witnessed a miracle—two miracles, in fact, but one is so much easier to recognize than the other. We can be so ignorant of the symptoms of our sinfulness, and the worse the inner turmoil and darkness, the harder it can be to see. "I'm not doing anything wrong, am I, am I really?" It might not seem so, but the bringing of ourselves, the worst of us as well as the best, to God, to Jesus, to this Son of Man, day after day, is so essential.

In our Sunday worship, when we are asked to confess our sins, I often fumble through any concise acknowledgement. "I guess I was kind of rude to that homeless guy out there on the street," I might say. "I was kind of annoyed that he was bothering me, looking for a buck." What about the bigger sin of not seeing the God in him? Or the God in myself?

That paralytic on the mat, lowered through the roof by his friends, had a chance to experience something extraordinary, something that is available to us all. Jesus is here to heal us, both body and soul.

REFLECTIONS FOR MODERN LIVING

- What is it that holds you back the most? Can you leave it with Jesus?
- Have you ever experienced any sort of divine healing?
- If you're struggling physically with some malady or disability, can you invite the Lord in to share in your struggle and bring God's healing?
- Do you ever turn to prayer even while getting the best medical help?

17

YOU CAN'T GROW IF YOUR MIND IS ALREADY MADE UP

We can all be pretty stubborn, avoiding any challenges to what we already believe. No one wants to see some deeply held "truth" suddenly turned upside down. The Pharisees, as we've seen, are often Jesus's principal adversaries in the Bible. Their way of thinking should be familiar to all of us, and alas, I daresay I sometimes act like them. You often see them trying to catch Jesus unaware, to trip him up, to disprove him. It would be too dangerous to have to welcome him into their hearts, to discover they were wrong.

Take the well-known incident of the coin—a well-greased coin, I'd say. In the Gospel of Mark, it is both Pharisees and Herodians, people who follow and worship Herod, king of the Jews, who challenge Jesus. They've already made their minds up and want to prove they're right. In the Gospel of Luke, the challengers are "spies" sent by the scribes and chief priests, Jesus's adversaries, tricksters.

At first, they slather Jesus with flattery and praise. "Teacher," they say, "we know that you are sincere, and show deference to no one; for you do not regard people with partiality but teach the way of God in accordance with truth." *Yes,*

yes, thank you very much, someone vainer than Jesus might say. *How kind of you to say all that. That is exactly who I am.* They want to lure him into their trap, put him to their holier-than-thou test. They ask the leading question, "Is it lawful to pay taxes to the emperor, or not? Should we pay them, or should we not?"

Looks like a setup. No matter how Jesus answers, he's going to invite trouble. If he says you should pay taxes, it'll look like he sides with the Roman rulers. If he says you shouldn't pay taxes, he'll seem to be a revolutionary, one of those protestors against Rome, sure to be punished (and how convenient would it be if the Roman rulers punished him? That way, these legalistic brothers of his own faith wouldn't have to do so themselves).

Of course, Jesus sees through their hypocrisy. More than just taking note of it, he chooses to reveal it to the others with a test. "Bring me a coin," he says, "and let me see it."

They bring one. "Whose head is on it," he asks, "and whose title?"

"The emperor's," they answer.

Jesus's reply goes down on the list of cleverest things anyone has ever said. "Give to the emperor the things that are the emperor's," he says, "and to God the things that are God's."

It's such a short answer and so rich with meaning that it has inspired reams of interpretation and analysis. Are the Caesars of our world granted their powers by God? Should we simply do as the government says, giving that material part of ourselves, our earnings, to government-sponsored plans, be they wars or tax plans that we don't quite approve of? Or are we simply to recoil from that because the things that are God's, our very being and existence, belong to God, and that's what's primary? Who do we worship, God or the temporal powers? We know what the answer should be—don't we?—but those coins themselves are easy to worship. Let me finger a few in my pocket.

Jesus has cleverly offered a paradox and riddle that is worth much consideration. Who is *my* Caesar? Where do *my* coins belong? I would like to imagine that his listeners went off and indulged in countless discussions to figure out what he meant. According to the biblical account, they were utterly amazed. Wouldn't you be? The best of them would now have a chance to change, if they dared.

On another occasion some of the Pharisees come to him and, once again, giving him a biblical query to catch him up, ask, "Is it lawful for a man to divorce his wife?" Ask Jesus a question, and he's going to shoot it right back at you with another question. "What did Moses command you?" he says, knowing full well what the answer will be. Then again, Jesus doesn't just preach, giving us a list of to-dos; he engages us in dialogue. That's how we grow. That's how we learn, if we can let go of any bit of rigid thinking on our part.

The Pharisees replied, pulling from Scripture, "Moses allowed a man to write a certificate of dismissal and to divorce her." Done.

But why did Moses do that? And what really would be the loving thing God might want? Jesus said to them, "Because of your hardness of heart he wrote this commandment for you." Jesus knows the trap they're setting, and he offers a beautiful image of what marriage can be and how it honors God richly, going right back to the Hebrew Bible, referencing it (if you're going to argue using Scripture, be prepared to get some Scripture back at you). "But from the beginning of creation, 'God made them male and female.' 'For this reason a man shall leave his father and mother and be joined to his wife, and the two shall become one flesh.' So they are no longer two, but one flesh."

He goes on to give us the line that illuminates many a marriage ceremony, "Therefore what God has joined together, let no one separate." (It makes me want to sing Noël Paul Stookey's "The Wedding Song," which I have indeed sung at several weddings. I once interviewed Stookey, and he explained how the song was completely heaven-sent. He needed to come up with a song to sing at the wedding of his fellow "Peter, Paul, and Mary" cohort Peter Yarrow, and the lyrics and tune came. Wow.)

In another instance, when the Pharisees were gathered, presumably to challenge him, Jesus started off by asking them the first question, "What do you think of the Messiah? Whose son is he?" (Matthew 22:42). No problem on this one. They knew the answer, pulling it from the Scripture they'd studied. "The son of David," they replied. But Jesus can dig just as deeply into Scripture, Bible passage arguing with Bible passage, verse versus verse. "How is it then that David by the Spirit calls him Lord?" He quotes from Psalm 110, verse one, where David, the putative author, says, "The Lord said to my Lord, 'Sit at my right hand, until I put your enemies under your feet.'" Jesus asks them, that if David called God Lord, how could David be God's son? God is Lord.

They are flummoxed. I might have been flummoxed, too, scratching my head to get the whole gist of the argument. The point is, it's a mind game, not an appeal to the heart. Clearly it is not by means of such linguistic tongue twisters or heady challenges that we are going to find and know God.

No one at the time could come up with a swift answer—as is often the case with Jesus's probing questions. They left unfulfilled. Or perhaps his probing and their unknowing would be the means to deeper, internal knowing. Isn't that all that Jesus wants? For us to know God? It can't ever happen if we're all too sure of ourselves.

REFLECTIONS FOR MODERN LIVING

- Are you open to hearing points of view that differ from your own? Are you willing to listen to any adversaries?
- Do you have any dark opinions that you secretly cling to?
- Is it possible to look for and find God's truth in places you didn't expect?
- How can you find inner change?

18

YOU ARE NEEDED

At Christmastime we have the joy of feasting on the Christmas story. We set up a crèche at home beneath the Christmas tree or on the windowsill to admire the figures. There they are, the shepherds who were watching their flock by night when the angel of the Lord appears, and they are "filled with fear."

I can't say the wooden figures in our crèche look too frightened. Maybe that's because they've been depicted *after* they've seen that heavenly vision and have dutifully made their way to the stable where Jesus lay so they can worship him. What they have done is trust a sublime vision and act on it.

Wouldn't you be afraid if an angel appeared to you out of the heavens when you were hard at work on your job, and the angel spoke to you, recognizing your fear right off, telling you not to be afraid (easier said than done)? This angel—this messenger—is delivering news that you'd think would go to the rich and powerful, all about the birth of the Messiah, the Christ, but no, the messenger has come to lowly *you* on the night shift. Even more shocking, the heavens managed to burst forth with more angels, enough to fill the sky, praising God

and promising peace. Peace. Don't we desperately need it now, and wasn't that so very true back then, some two thousand years ago?

I've always admired the shepherds for doing what they were told. They had a place to go to and a message to bring, one they'd never forget. They might have left one or two of their own behind to stay with the sheep, or perhaps they entrusted an angel or two to look after the sheep while they were gone. A stable with a manger was their kind of place, their comfort zone. Much better than being asked to go to a glittery palace where they'd have to rent expensive clothes—going deep into debt—before they could even walk in the door. Here they went dressed as they were. The musty cloak and crook would do just fine.

If they had distrusted the messenger, they never would have gone, but the sight was so thrilling that when they returned to the fields, they couldn't stop praising and glorifying God. They had to share what they had been told about this child. The mother of the baby would never forget any of it, treasuring their words, pondering them in her heart.

What an extraordinary thing. God came down to us as a little child. That's what we celebrate at Christmas. God has become one of us, and he doesn't start this earthly journey by becoming a popular jock or a glittering movie star but a baby, a mewling, fidgeting, sleeping, hungry child, born in the humblest of circumstances. Look who its earthly parents are, a young woman and a carpenter. Why would God do it this way? What are we supposed to understand? In words that my son, Reverend Tim, emphasized in a Christmas sermon when his own daughter was just two months old, the story is a reminder that God needs us. God needs us to survive.

I'll never forget the church Christmas pageant some years ago when a twelve-year-old girl was playing Mary—one of my Sunday school students—and reenacted the scene of the Annunciation. The angel Gabriel appeared to her and told her the extraordinary news that she would give birth to the Savior, and that he would be called Jesus. She goes to call on her cousin Elizabeth, who in her old age is also expecting a child, one that leaps with joy in Elizabeth's womb. It is then that Mary goes on to chant or sing or say what we call the Magnificat, a profound poem of joy magnifying God and proclaiming some of the amazing things that will be done because of this yet unborn child.

"My soul magnifies the Lord, and my spirit rejoices in God my Savior," she sings or says, "for he has looked with favor on the lowliness of his servant. Surely, from now on all generations will call me blessed . . ."

It's not an easy text, and I've always wondered how Mary could possibly have come up with it, until that pageant Sunday when this twelve-year-old girl, dressed as Mary, walked down the center aisle of church, uttering all those words without any hesitation or stumbling. *That could have been Mary*, I thought, a young woman gifted by God.

The Christmas pageant and the rough-hewn crèche, what poignant reminders of the roles we are asked to play. Most years at church the holy child is a little doll held in the arms of his mother, wrapped in white or lying in a manger. There have been times that the baby was an actual infant, and then everybody could hold their breath. Would it call out? Would it cry? Would it know how to be quiet during the singing?

If you've had a baby or held a baby—like Reverend Tim and us that Christmas—you know what it is like. How vulnerable the child is, how needy, how often it needs to be fed, how often it must be changed, how vulnerable we feel trying to satisfy its very needs and understand its various wants. Why is the baby crying? Does it need to be fed again? Is it cold? Is it tired? Does it need to sleep? Should we change the diaper again? Why, on earth, would God in all his power choose to come down like this? Take it as a reminder—thanks, Reverend Tim—that God needs us.

Our kids, when they were young, played different roles in the pageant over the years. When our older son, Will, was barely out of diapers, he was part of that heavenly chorus, leaping down the aisle with uncontainable joy, his diaphanous wings trembling, his tinfoil halo barely staying on. I can picture him as one of the wise men, in later years, carrying one of those treasured gifts on a pillow, a terrycloth camel hobbling after. They were sheep some years, baaing down the aisle; they were shepherds carrying crooks. They had roles to play, and as parents, gazing on in admiration and wonder at the talents that could pull such a thing off, we felt ourselves called into roles, all around that little baby who needed us.

God needs us.

When I taught in Sunday school, I liked to test my students' knowledge—okay, it was a setup—about who gathered around the baby Jesus, knowing that someone would mention "the three kings." Some could even quote a line from "We Three Kings." Then I'd have them go back to the text in Matthew. "Where does it say three?" I'd ask. And are they ever called kings? All it says is "wise men from the East," or *magi*, to use the Greek. Let them see if they could stump their parents. The tradition of three comes from the three gifts they were bearing, I went on to explain (Mr. Nerdy Teacher), gold, frankincense, and myrrh. There could have been two of them or five or six or twenty, and how did they get there? I could ask. They followed a star, having been told of a child who was born to be king of the Jews.

They went to Jerusalem first, where the real king was reigning, wise/mad King Herod. He got all the experts together, the chief priests and teachers of the law, and asked the experts where this so-called king—this apparent challenge to his own power—might be found. Bethlehem, they tell him, consulting the ancient texts, news he passes on to the wise men, with malicious intent. When these wise men from the east—who obviously learned enough to follow some celestial sign—locate this child/king, would they come back and tell King Herod so he could worship it too? They agreed. But then, who would say no to Herod?

The star takes them to their destination, pausing right there in the sky. If the wise men had come from as far away as Persia or even farther, they would have been traveling for months on end, perhaps leaving before Jesus was even born, called ahead of time, carrying their gifts. They brought the gifts out of their treasure chests and presented them to the child. Here was a child who needed all the help they could get, especially if their very existence could be threatened by the temporal power of an envious, vain, violent king.

Warned in a dream, the wise men didn't go back through Jerusalem, but returned home a different way, avoiding Herod, with a subtle spiritual point: How could they possibly have taken the same route home after what they had seen?

Warned in a dream himself by the appearance of an angel, Joseph is told to get away and flee to Egypt with the child, because Herod wants to destroy the infant. They are to stay in Egypt until he is told it is safe to return.

The part of the story that is never acted out in any Christmas pageant I've ever seen is what Herod does next, the terrible monstrous thing, something that the historical Herod, as described in other sources, might very well have done. Violent and tyrannical, he is furious and has all the children age two and under in and around Bethlehem slaughtered. God's enemies are willing to go to any end if they feel threatened. It is no wonder that God needs us. God needs you.

That story resolves in another dream. When this King Herod finally dies, an angel appears in a dream to Joseph in Egypt and tells him that it is now safe to take the mother and child back to Israel. The one who was trying to kill him is dead. With the warning of one more dream to avoid Herod's son, Joseph takes a route of safety to Galilee, where the family will make its home in Nazareth.

The Slaughter of the Innocents doesn't make for a pretty scene, let alone something I'd want to see my grandkids act out, yet it's an important part of the story, especially as it relates to the senseless violence we have experienced in our own times. Are there not too many innocent victims attacked in our world? Scroll through the heartbreaking headlines and see for yourself.

It's easy enough to view the story through the lens of prophecy and foreshadowing, the flight in Egypt a resonant reminder of the Israelites' flight into Egypt, where another Joseph followed, and then Moses rescued them. The birth stories of Jesus are full of myth, but to call something a myth doesn't mean it isn't true in the deepest sense of the word. Indeed, I believe that God can speak to us in dreams today, like the ones that the wise men and Joseph heeded, warning us and guiding us in God's good way.

God might have come to us first as a child, but the message resonates deeply. God needs us now more than ever.

Reflections for Modern Living

- What particular gifts do you have that the world needs and God needs?
- Is there a role in the Christmas story that you identify with?
- Have you ever experienced a message from God that came in a dream?
- Do you look to the heavens, the creation, to follow the stars the Creator sends?

19

BE GOOD SOIL

My mom was blessed with abundant curiosity. When she heard of something, she wanted to know more. She asked questions. She listened carefully. She was compassionate. We kids grew used to hearing her on the phone, listening patiently to her friends with lots of "Ohs" and "Ah-has" and "Awwwws." If she learned of something sad, she shook her head and sometimes cried. Blessedly uncomplicated, she defended people who deserved to be defended. I remember people hounding her with unkind questions when her beloved tennis partner left an unhappy marriage. Mom refused to go with them in their quest for gossip, cutting them off.

As a child, if I had something special to share—a story, a picture, a song I had learned, something from a book I'd read—I could go to her and share it, certain that she would match my delight. When I was hurt and wanted to cry, I knew she would embrace me and hold me tight through my tears.

She was good soil, nurturing her four children almost unconsciously. We had been planted, and she wanted us to grow. She knew there were challenges ahead, and roadblocks, but as long as we dug deep, holding onto her love, we would survive and flourish, our roots well grounded. She didn't preach her faith—she rarely talked about it. She lived it.

I think of her when Jesus talks about the sower who went out to sow seed. A longtime city dweller, what do I know about farming? But even living in an apartment I have seen what it is to plant bulbs in pots with fertile soil and move them around in pots to catch the light, watering them and trimming them, delighting in the buds that burst open and bloom.

I yearn to sow, following my mom's example. That means being full of curiosity, wanting to know about lives that are far different from mine, stepping into a cab and reading the driver's name, asking at the start where they might be from, or noting the pictures behind a receptionist's desk and asking about that cute kid with the ball or the girl holding the doll. Are those your kids or grandkids? How old are they? What do they like to do? God forbid if I seem tiresome.

The opportunities to be good soil are legion. We must take heed and do all we can to be nurturing souls. In our families, with our children and grandchildren, our nieces and nephews, with our friends, with complete strangers, we have the chance to make a better, joy-filled, kinder world.

Lest I forget, my dad did the same too. He couldn't get into an elevator without chatting up whoever else was there—at least if the person looked willing to chat. He might not have remembered the names of someone's children or grandchildren, but he would never fail to ask about them, noting some little fact he *had* remembered: "How is your daughter doing in college?" "What does your son think of his new job?" "We loved those pictures of you in your Christmas card."

And at the close of any conversation with us kids, he always proclaimed, "I'm proud of you." Every letter or long-distance call he signed off with "Love ya." His prayers at the dinner table, the extemporaneous graces he said full of the news of the day—the six o'clock news, a friend dubbed them—inevitably included a petition or two for us kids, the test we were studying for, the drill team auditions, the upcoming piano recital. He'd close with "Bless this food to our use and us to thy service," with a sure inclusion of Mom, "and bless the hands that have prepared it." Then Mom's much-blessed hands would dish out the casserole.

Jesus believes we have the power to nurture the word, his message, in the good soil of our faith. We can become good soil. He tells a story to make his point, a parable recorded in the three synoptic Gospels, Matthew, Mark, and Luke. In the Mark version, we learn that there was a big crowd gathered around Jesus, so he stepped into a boat and sat there, with the people listening from the shore as he told his tale, the lake making it easier for all to see him, and in my imagination, it resonates with the words.

The sower sets out to sow the seeds, a bit aimlessly but then, that's part of Jesus's point (like I've said, one of the lures of Jesus's stories, and any good story for that matter, is that you often find multiple messages ready to speak to you). Some of the seed falls on the path where the birds come and eat it. Some of the seed falls on rocky ground without much soil. It sprouts up quickly but because of the thin soil it can't send down deep roots, and when the sun comes up it withers away.

Then there are the seeds that fall among thorns—thorny plants, I presume—and when they grow up, they choke the seed, and it never grows enough to produce grain. But fortunately, there are seeds that fall into good, rich soil, and they bring forth grain, increasing thirty-, sixty-, hundredfold—mind you, the sort of vivid detail his rustic farming and fishing folk would have grasped immediately. After all, many of them would have had to gather up grain in the fields at harvest time.

What is the message? "Let anyone with ears to hear listen," Jesus says cryptically. It is not for us to go for the quick Wikipedia summary that x means x and y means y. We need to hear the story and consider how it relates to us. How might we be good soil? Later, when he is with the disciples, they ask him about parables. They are confused. Why does Jesus talk that way? He explains that they have been given the secret of God's kingdom—it's standing or sitting right in front of them. But for others, those on the outside, the parables are a riddle wrapped in a mystery inside an enigma (to borrow Winston Churchill's words). Hold the big picture in your head. This is not a lesson in farming. It goes deeper.

I once heard a preacher say that the biblical explanations of the parables, coming out of Jesus's mouth, might have been later additions to the text. Maybe, maybe not. They don't read like CliffsNotes or a quick sermon summary. They have that same quality of the parables, giving his disciples—and us—something to ponder. As Jesus explains, referring to those on the outside, "They may indeed look, but not perceive, and may indeed listen, but not understand," apparently a reference to a line from the book of Isaiah, followed by words that move me, "so that they may not turn again and be forgiven" (this is the Mark version). That's what it's about, isn't it? Knowing how we need to turn to God when we've failed, as we inevitably do.

Who is the sower? He is the one sowing the word of God. I especially appreciate in church *hearing* the word in worship. We read, read, read all the time, but—to repeat myself—for centuries the Scriptures were primarily passed along by being heard. Someone read the words aloud, and everyone else listened. They were a group gathered, whether in church or someone's home. There's a power to hearing something in community. Being made aware of the distractions can be part of it. "Wait, wait . . . what did you say?" *Wait, wait, what did Jesus say?*

"These are the ones on the path where the word is sown," Jesus says, explaining this parable. "When they hear, Satan immediately comes and takes away the word that is sown in them." Perhaps it's because of some dogged determination to follow their own prescribed path that the word can't bloom or even take root. Satan, here, can stand for all sorts of wrong thinking, snatching words of truth from our perception before we're even aware of it. Evil loves its disguises.

Jesus goes on to decode the meaning of seeds sown on rocky ground: "When they hear the word, they immediately receive it with joy. But they have no root and endure only for a while; then, when trouble or persecution arises on account of the word, immediately they fall away." Take note of what distracts them, trouble in their journey. Their faith doesn't run deep enough, rooted as it is in rocky soil, to withstand the suffering that life can bring, especially for those early followers who were going against cultural and religious norms. But then, can't a brazen, faith-based statement attract trouble and persecution in our own secular era, even from those who feel they know exactly what God demands of them?

There are the seeds sown among the thorns. "These are the ones who hear the word," Jesus says, "but the cares of the world, and the lure of wealth, and the desire for other things come in and choke the word, and it yields nothing." How hard it can be to hold on to the word when there are so many other "words" out there, seemingly justified by glossy success, screaming out for our attention. Our conscious and unconscious desires make choices influenced by glamorous images that bounce across our phones and TV screens. "Yes, Lord, I do want to pray, but let me watch this first." Thorns don't necessarily have to look like thorns; that's the thorny business of life.

At last, there is the promise given to us when we "hear the word and accept it and bear fruit," an unimaginable bounty, increasing "thirty- and sixty- and a hundredfold," all from something as small as a seed of grain planted in the ground. Note, it's not just a matter of hearing the word, but accepting it—opening yourself up to its every call—and then seeing it bear fruit. There is deep joy infused in this kind of person. You want to hear them, listen to them, have them listen to you. They are—as we can be—good soil.

Reflections for Modern Living

- How do you nurture your soul to be like the rich, fertile soil Jesus speaks of?
- What distracts you from hearing the word and following the word?
- Do you have any models you turn to for living a rich, spiritual life?
- What are the things that help you dig deep spiritually, like Bible study, regular prayer, or volunteer work?

20

Jesus Weeps for You and with You

It's the shortest verse in the Bible, only two words: "Jesus wept," two words that speak volumes.

Lazarus, the brother of Martha and Mary—she who would pour perfume on Jesus and wipe his feet with her hair—was sick, and so the sisters sent word to Jesus, knowing of course that he could heal the sick one. Jesus with his ability to see both present, past, and future, knows where this event is going, and announces that Lazarus's sickness will not end in death. On the contrary, it will be for God's glory, "so that God's Son may be glorified through it," a statement that sounds like a stirring drumroll or theme song at the opening of a movie.

Jesus loved Martha and her sister, Mary, but he did not rush off to their home in Bethany right away, staying instead an extra two days where he was, scripting, in a way, the miracle that would happen. When he and the disciples finally head out, he tells them, "Our friend Lazarus has fallen asleep; but I am going there to awaken him." *Our friend.* What a lovely way to include him in the fold. The disciples figure that if their friend is asleep, that means he'll get better, right? Jesus repeats himself and says it very plainly this time, "Lazarus is dead."

Dreadful news it must be. However, Jesus indicates that he was glad not to be there at the sick man's bedside, "so that you may believe," a hint of what is to come.

By the time they get to Bethany, Lazarus had been in the tomb for four days—no quick update by phone or text—and the mourners had gathered around Martha and Mary to comfort them. Martha rushes out to meet Jesus, saying that if only he had been there her brother would not have died. Martha exhibits an unhesitant faith in Jesus, as is often the case with the women in the Gospels, a wake-up call for any of us know-it-all dudes. "Your brother will rise again," Jesus says. She thinks he means some sort of resurrection at the end of time, giving Jesus the chance to remind her who he is and why he's come, a bumper-sticker announcement as well as an invitation: "I am the resurrection and the life. Those who believe in me, even though they die, will live, and everyone who lives and believes in me will never die." Does she believe this?

Of course she does. She reiterates her faith, holds on to it, the kind of thing that is especially helpful at trying moments: "Yes, Lord," she says, "I believe that you are the Messiah, the Son of God, the one coming into the world." She goes and fetches her sister, Mary, who is followed by some of the other mourners. When Mary reaches Jesus, she falls at his feet—a physical expression of her faith—and says, "Lord, if you had been here, my brother would not have died." Jesus sees her weeping and the others weeping and is both deeply moved and troubled.

"Where have you laid him?" he asks. It's not like he doesn't know, but this feels like one of those questions Jesus asks to engage his listeners—and us.

"Come and see, Lord," they say.

Come and see, Lord. A refrain for life, a prayer for all our days.

Then comes that profound two-word biblical verse: "Jesus wept."

It is almost enough to stop right there. Jesus is about to perform an astounding miracle, one he has set up from the beginning, bringing back to life a man who has been dead for four days, the beloved brother of two of his dedicated followers. And yet, before he puts all that goodness to work, he feels the pain of those mourning and participates in it.

Jesus knows what we're going through. Jesus knows our sorrow. Jesus knows our pain and can feel it. He cries with us. Our prayers are not ascending to a distant, abstract being. Think of how comforting it can be to sit with someone who feels your pain and doesn't try to talk you out of it but can cry for you and with you. Indeed, Jesus could have reminded Martha and Mary and those mourners, "Enough with the tears. Focus on this miracle I'm about to do." But no, the miracle doesn't come without empathy and compassion. Some have even suggested that Jesus wept for Lazarus because of the sadness he'd face being called back from the glories of eternity. Whatever reason, Jesus wept.

The mourners note Jesus's tears. "See how he loved him," they say. Others wonder why this man who could cure a blind man didn't keep Lazarus from dying. Still deeply moved, Jesus comes to the tomb where a stone was laid across the entrance, very much like the stone that will be laid across the entrance to Jesus's tomb—and found removed on Easter day. I don't think it's foreshadowing as much as reminding us that God is present in past, present, and future. Godly time merges together.

Jesus tells them to take away the stone. Martha is not so sure, despite her faithfulness. She reminds Jesus of the bad odor that would come from a body rotting in a tomb for four days, as though Jesus is so otherworldly he would forget the gruesome details of everyday life and death. Jesus prods her again to hold on to her faith. "Did I not tell you that if you believed, you would see the glory of God?" Note to self: Miracles come to those who believe.

They take away the stone and Jesus looks up, addressing himself to God the Father. "Father, I thank you for having heard me. I knew that you always hear me, but I have said this for the sake of the crowd standing here, so that they may believe that you sent me." To be seen and not just heard. "Lazarus," he commands in a loud voice. "Come out!"

The dead man comes out, his hands and feet wrapped with strips of linen, and a cloth around his face. Jesus said to them, "Unbind him and let him go." What vivid imagery. We all need to take off the fearful attire of death and live, truly live.

Lazarus was dead and now he lives.

REFLECTIONS FOR MODERN LIVING

- Do you ever cry when you pray or pray when you cry?
- Does loneliness ever hit you, even in the midst of a thousand emails and text messages?
- Have you been through times of loss and mourning only to be reassured of God's presence?
- How has God comforted you during a trying time in your life?

21

Be extravagant in love

Jesus shocked those around him by not behaving according to the dictates of society. I believe he means for us to take risks too, especially out of love and compassion and care. To love your neighbor as yourself might mean shaking things up for some of your neighbors. The ones who get it will get it. How else can we change the world unless we reach out to those who feel especially unloved?

As we've seen, the Pharisees are often depicted in the Gospels as Jesus's adversaries, his challengers, because their power was challenged, their reputation was being threatened. Then again, Jesus could just as easily dine with them and welcome them as followers, even if they felt they could only come to him in the middle of the night.

I have a picture over my desk, a copy of one of my favorite paintings that shows how one of those Pharisees, Nicodemus, came to Jesus in the middle of the night, the safest time to approach him without being noticed. He would ask Jesus endless questions, stepping away from his role in society and following an inner urge. In the painting, by the artist Henry Ossawa Tanner, the two of them are on a moonlit rooftop, Nicodemus with a long white beard, leaning forward, Jesus illuminated by warm firelight coming up from the stairs.

Nicodemus calls Jesus Rabbi without any of the other Pharisees' apparent back-handed manipulation. He wants to learn. Right away he gets language that has enhanced followers of Jesus ever since. "No one can see the kingdom of God without being born from above," Jesus tells him, describing what it means to be born anew. "Born again" is the phrase we often hear, an opportunity for us. Baffled, Nicodemus goes straight ahead looking for some literal explanation. Born anew? How could anyone be born after growing old, re-entering their mother's womb, he wonders. It doesn't make any sense.

Good luck with that kind of thinking. Jesus goes on to challenge him with mystical language that must have made Nicodemus's head spin. It does mine. And yet, isn't that Jesus's very point? We can't reach him, we can't find God, we can't understand these profound things by being literal-minded. Being born from above means being born of the Spirit. "The wind blows where it chooses, and you hear the sound of it, but you do not know where it comes from or where it goes. So it is with everyone who is born of the Spirit," Jesus says. (I had a colleague who would turn to this phrase—playfully—to describe another colleague's unpredictability; you could never know where the wind blows.)

"If I have told you about earthly things and you do not believe, how can you believe if I tell you about heavenly things?" Jesus asks.

Think of all the earthly miracles Jesus has performed. And now Nicodemus's nighttime visit gives Jesus the chance to offer a summary of his calling. It's the one Bible verse that people best remember, chapter and verse, John 3:16: "For God so loved the world that he gave his only Son, so that everyone who believes in him may not perish but may have eternal life." I love being reminded of its context. Who was he speaking to? A late-night visitor, like me or you. Savor that, Nicodemus.

The passage is repeated so often that it can lose some of its transcendent power. Then again, I know a man who when he saw other college kids like himself holding up signs at a ball game that said "John 3:16," he figured it was a reference to some team's score. Nevertheless, it got him searching, delving deep into Scripture for the first time. Perhaps it worked its mysterious power because after much investigation, discernment, and prayer, he went on to seminary and became a minister.

Beware, Jesus can change the course of your life, as he did for Nicodemus. The man, apparently transformed by that secret visit, makes two more crucial appearances in the Gospel of John. First, when the Pharisees were agitating against Jesus, asking why the temple police didn't arrest Jesus, Nicodemus speaks up to his fellow Pharisees, reminding them that their law "does not judge people without first giving them a hearing to find out what they are doing, does it?"

Then, even more poignantly, he showed up at Jesus's burial, digging into his deep pockets to provide about a hundred pounds of myrrh and aloes for the body, which he and Joseph of Arimathea, another secret disciple of Jesus, used as they wrapped the body with the spices in linen cloths and lay him in the tomb. Myrrh might be familiar to you as one of the three gifts the wise men brought to Jesus as a newborn babe, a prefiguration of the Lord's untimely end.

Nicodemus took risks to show his love. He went outside his circle, beyond his comfort zone, facing possible rejection from his group, even after Jesus's brutal death, when there could have been little hope or promise in being a follower of Jesus. It didn't stop him. "Oh, love that will not let me go . . ." to quote the words of a beloved hymn.

For another extravagant display of love, I think of the woman who anointed Jesus's feet or head (the accounts differ) with costly perfume or oil. In three of the Gospels, it happens shortly before the Last Supper and irritates some of the disciples, who question the extravagant display, asking why the ointment wasn't sold instead and the money given to the poor. Get your priorities right, right? But Jesus applauds her gesture and notes that the poor will always abound whereas he will not be around much longer.

"She has anointed my body before its burial" (even before what Nicodemus did). He promises that what she has done will be retold and remembered whenever his story is told. In the Gospel of John, she is identified by name, Mary the sister of Martha.

In Luke the incident seems to happen earlier, when a Pharisee invites Jesus into his house to eat with him (once again, Jesus meeting with the wrong people, his apparent adversaries—not the sort of thing you see much in contemporary politics). There a woman, a so-called sinner, comes, bringing an alabaster jar of expensive ointment. She weeps at his feet, bathing them with her tears, kissing them and then anointing them with the ointment.

The Pharisee is shocked. Shouldn't Jesus have known what kind of woman this was, touching him and kissing him? Jesus responds with a parable, once again about money. Maybe it's because when you put these things in financial terms, we're more likely to get the point. Don't our heads often revert to money? Jesus describes two debtors, one who owes five hundred denarii (a denarius was about a day's wage for a laborer) and the other only fifty. When they couldn't pay, the creditor canceled both of their debts. "Now which of them will love him more?" Jesus asks. Simon the Pharisee answers, supposing it would be the one with the greater debt.

Bingo. "You have judged rightly," Jesus says. Still, he doesn't let Simon off the hook. After all, Simon didn't wash Jesus's feet with water or kiss him or anoint his head with oil, whereas she bathed his feet with her tears and dried them with her hair, anointing them with oil. "Her sins, which were many, have been forgiven," he says. Was that what she expected? That he would tell her that her sins are forgiven, as he does? I don't think so. She's not looking for any bargains. It's not a visit of quid pro quo. She enters the Pharisee's house, coming to Jesus with an expression of unfathomable love, and an investment in it, all of which pays off. The gift is reciprocated multiple times.

"The one to whom little is forgiven," Jesus says, "loves little." Not this woman, about whom he says, "Your faith has saved you; go in peace."

The differing stories, the various accounts, the named and unnamed figures, they all merge for me into one overall message. Be big. Love Jesus. Know how wrong you are and have been wrong at times and know how forgiveness is there in wait for you. Especially when you match it with love.

Reflections for Modern Living

- Have you ever asked someone privately about their faith or let them ask you?
- What is the most extravagant way you can think of expressing your love of God?
- Can you think of a modern equivalent for bathing someone's feet?
- Is being born anew in the spirit something that can happen again and again?

22

Change Comes from the Inside

Let's go straight to a quote from the Bible, something Jesus said: "Woe to you, scribes and Pharisees, hypocrites! For you clean the outside of the cup and of the plate, but inside they are full of greed and self-indulgence. You blind Pharisee! First clean the inside of the cup, so that the outside also may become clean." Clean those insides first.

It's all too tempting to claim that I'm not at all like those nasty, hypocritical scribes and Pharisees. They put their goodness on display, dressing the part, acting the part, expecting appreciation and reverence wherever they go. They yearn for admiration and expect it all around. After all, their supposed holiness has come with a lot of work—don't you know it? They study the Scriptures diligently, tirelessly. They worship endlessly, focusing on every tiny iota of law and practice, setting themselves apart from others, seeing themselves as better, and showing it, expecting to be worthy of imitation and praise. But has all that work and effort made any difference to their real selves?

A lot can be said for "going through the motions." You know, writing that thank-you note, sending that card, writing

that check, showing up at that difficult moment, apologizing for something you did, speaking out or holding back, being nice, acting nice, but how much does it matter who you become and who you are if it is "only going through the motions?"

The question is: Who are you going through the motions for, yourself or just how it looks to others?

Transformation does not come easy, and if you're truly engaged, you need to look to your motives. What are they? Who are you trying to impress? What do you want to make of yourself?

I'm grateful for the many hours I've worked in an office with gifted colleagues, even if it there were times it all seemed part of the daily grind. Heck, wasn't there at least a paycheck every two weeks to make me feel the effort was worthwhile, not to mention health insurance and some bucks to go into my retirement account?

One of the things I am especially grateful for, looking back, are those tough times when things *didn't* go so smoothly and I was truly challenged. A challenge to your authority, a challenge to your self-image is a valuable thing. At least it was for me. I had to look inside to see who I was and who I wanted to be.

Without going too much into the details, I can think of some occasions when I truly failed and, most important, was called on it. In a work situation when something comes up on a review or a one-on-one confab with your boss or colleague, you want to do everything in your power to prove that no, you're not that apparent failure someone thought you were or that you didn't really do anything wrong or that you are all too ready to be quick with the apology. "I'm so, so sorry," you say. "I didn't mean to hurt your feelings." Well, you know the things that come to mind. You might say as much to a neighbor or a friend. God only knows you probably need to say it to your spouse.

What I'm grateful for is that my work compatriots made me dig deeper, and in one instance even work with an outside resource, to understand what they were talking about and how to change. I needed to change from the inside if I was ever going to grow.

I would say that's a thousand times truer of a marriage relationship. With a spouse, if you're truly being honest with each other, you can't get away with simply cleaning the outside of the cup. Just pretending isn't going to last for long. The person you live with will see through you. It can be very painful at times, but I think that's one of the gifts of marriage. You're being given the chance to grow. I can talk too much, can be too proud of myself, can forget to listen carefully, can lose track of compassion, can learn how I fail in ways I never perceived. For example—to take something lighthearted—my bride said on our honeymoon, "Don't you ever use a napkin?" And it wasn't just the outside of the cup she was calling attention to. I mean, I was so busy telling a story or maybe retelling a story she'd probably heard a half dozen times already, that I didn't pay attention to what was going through her mind.

How will I live with a guy who never uses a napkin?

With my now adult children we've cut a deal: "Dad," says my older son, William, "if we've heard the story at least seven times, we'll let you know."

Is it possible that one of the gifts of marriage and the gift of family is to discover how much you really need to be forgiven, how much you are failing? Painful and transformative at the same time.

The Pharisees were spiritual show-offs, and nothing can be more dangerous. They were painstakingly observant, but it didn't make much difference, because even doing their good deeds it was mostly about being seen by others. We have many ways of recognizing and rewarding good behavior, with awards and lists and honors. They can all make us feel better, that we're encouraging goodness and honoring it. And yet, isn't there greater power to be found in doing your good deeds—whatever they might be—in secret and expecting nothing in return? I'm all too ready to let our accountant know about every charitable donation we've made, just to get that tax deduction—can you blame me?—but wouldn't it be better if I didn't even write it down here?

See.

One of the keys to my spiritual growth and living is a dedicated time in the morning of prayer and meditation. If you looked at me and saw my face, my eyes closed, my hands in my lap, a Bible or prayer book not far away, you might think that my head is full of holy thoughts one hundred percent of the time. You would be wrong. I generally use a sacred word or image to ground my thoughts and meditation, but inevitably a thousand distractions come into my head. I think about a meeting I need to prep for, or someone I should email, or some writing assignment I might have, or some bills that need to be paid—and do we have enough in our account to cover them? How holy is that?

And yet, I would argue that paying attention to all those niggling worries and concerns is part of the process. I'm discovering what's going on inside. Not for nothing is it called mindfulness. I subscribe to the practice of what is sometimes called "catch and release." In my case it's a matter of catching the thought and releasing it to God. It's the only way I can conceive of growing—changing from the inside. It can be truly humbling. But then, less *is* more.

As Jesus said, "All who exalt themselves will be humbled, and those who humble themselves will be exalted." Welcome those occasions and circumstances that humble you. They might just be chances to change and grow.

REFLECTIONS FOR MODERN LIVING

- What way do you most yearn to change?
- Do you agree with that old saying "no pain, no gain"?
- If you practiced "catch and release" in prayer, what would you most like to release to God?
- How would you like best to be remembered?

23

Everyone Counts

It's easy enough to feel like you don't really matter in this world, in the larger scheme of things or in the smaller. Who am I? What does it matter what I say or think? Why would anyone care? Who would want to listen to me, little old me?

Ours is a culture that celebrates luminaries. We look for stars in the firmament. We are drawn to famous figures. Think of the thrill that comes over you if you just happen to pass some famous actor or sports figure or fashion model. (I'll never forget walking past Whoopi Goldberg.) How clever you would be if you caught a snapshot on your phone and managed to post it. Think of all the likes you might accumulate. Imagine all the flattering emojis. Gosh, you might even get more "friends" following you. As an author, to promote any book—God forbid it might be this one—I've been told I should have thousands of followers. That would certainly be more followers than Jesus had in his lifetime. Thank you, Jesus. How amazing that Jesus managed to make such a difference with only those chosen twelve, and a few more, those women in particular, as we've seen.

Is it any wonder that Jesus took pains to remind them and the rest of us how much each one of us counted?

There is the story Jesus told of the lost sheep, something that probably registered more deeply with that pastoral culture than ours. Jesus even frames it as a question, "Which one of you, having a hundred sheep and losing one of them, does not leave the ninety-nine in the wilderness and go after the one that is lost until he finds it?"

Imagine that challenge—and that risk. All those other sheep lingering in the wilderness where they could be attacked by a wild beast or face some grueling atmospheric event or perhaps plunderers looking for food and hides. The shepherd hunts far and near to find that one lost sheep, carrying it home on his shoulders, calling all his friends and neighbors together to celebrate. What was lost has been found. I can see Sunday school images of the little lamb found among brambles, rocks, and thorns, being picked up, cuddled and carried, fed and nurtured.

You are it. I am it. From the exterior there might be nothing seemingly "lost sheep" about me. Happily married, a good career, involved in my church, thrilled to be a dad, recently gifted with grandkids—wow—but there have been and continue to be "lost sheep" moments in my life, when I don't feel connected to God, when the Lord feels far away, when I'm wondering if I'm doing the right thing, when I fear I've failed as a husband or a dad or a colleague. There have been traumatic health issues when I wondered why I was being punished—it could feel like punishment—after trying to do the right healthy things. Geez, God, haven't I been good about getting regular exercise? What is it about my diet that might have invited or promoted that "not normal" blood test?

When you're a lost sheep, you're not sure you really count. You can't imagine that you're really missed. You don't think you're worthy of being rescued. You want to blame yourself. You feel unloved. Worse than that, you feel unlovable. You could die alone from the loneliness and the cold. You can't imagine that anyone would miss you. If they could only know how bad you feel.

Jesus is quick to tip the balance in your favor. The one who needs help the most is far more important than the ninety-nine. It almost seems as though all of them can be sacrificed for the lost one. And yet, aren't those ninety-nine also being looked after by God while the shepherd—the Shepherd—searches for and finds that single lost sheep?

As if that story is not enough to make the point, Jesus also tells of the woman who loses one of ten silver coins. She lights a lamp, sweeps the house, and does everything she can to find it. Jesus understands how money speaks to us. Well, wouldn't you do everything in your power to recover some lost funds? After all, it's a silver coin, not a copper penny. It's worth the effort. For me it would be like losing my phone—worth its weight in gold. How will I contact anybody? How will I respond to a text? How will I get the news? How will I listen to a podcast? How will anybody contact me? At least technology has given us that "Find My" feature, but then you need a phone to use it. You need to borrow someone's unlost phone. (Prayer would seem to be our own spiritual mechanism for "Find My.")

And then famously when it comes to lost souls, in the Gospel of Luke, he launches into the story of the Prodigal Son. It might be better renamed the story of the Prodigal Father, seeing as it shows God's prodigal love.

There are two sons, and the younger one asks for all his inheritance so he can go live the high life—squandering every cent. Think of the parties, the women, the drinking, the drugs, the luxurious attire, the expensive places to stay. It all might have felt worthwhile at the time, but the money goes too fast, and all too soon he is working as a hired hand, feeding the pigs with food that he wished he could eat himself, filling his empty stomach and soul. He thought back to what he'd left. His father's hired hands were better off than he was.

He drags himself home, no doubt hopeless and distraught. You might expect his father to wag a finger at the fellow and say, "Didn't I tell you? Why on earth did you waste all that money? I'm going to put you to work now." Instead, the dad welcomes back the wayward son with open arms and compassion, and the son expresses his deep remorse. The celebration at his return is greater than he could possibly have imagined. The finest robe is brought for him (no doubt to cover up his torn and dirty garments), a ring for his finger, sandals for his feet, and the fatted calf killed for the welcome-home feast. "For this son of mine was dead and is alive again," the father says. "He was lost and is found!"

It's easy enough to sympathize with the elder brother who comes home and hears the music and the dancing, learns of the fatted calf being killed—one that he had probably spent time feeding and taking care of—and the return of his prodigal brother. I would be mighty angry, too, asking myself, asking my father, why I never got a party like this after doing all the right things, slaving away, working my fingers to the bone. What kind of thanks did I get? Where's *my* party? Okay, Jesus, what's the point? What's the message?

"Son," the father says, "you are always with me, and all that is mine is yours. But we had to celebrate and rejoice, because this brother of yours was dead and has come to life; he was lost and has been found."

The older son hasn't been in a spiritual place that would allow him to accept God's prodigal love. I can imagine him feeling smug and self-congratulatory, all that work after his brother left. He'd always thought he was better, and hasn't he proved it? Let that wastrel be gone, may the fool get what he deserves. But here just desserts are thrown upside down. The older brother hasn't allowed himself an ounce of love and compassion, only the narrowest of anger and pride. Who is the sinner here? The one who longs for God and forgiveness or the one who doesn't have any room for it?

God loves them both. They both count. And to see the world with God's eyes is to love every lost sheep and yearn for their return to the fold.

You count. Come on home. Even if you think you never left. It's a better place than you could ever expect.

Reflections for Modern Living

- Do you ever feel you don't really matter, even to God?
- When have you felt lost only to be found?
- Who are the lost sheep in today's world?
- Which of the two sons in the parable of the prodigal son do you most identify with?

24

Hang out with Jesus

If asked what I believe, I like to say I'm a follower of Jesus, or at least I try to be. But what on earth does that mean? And why would I say that? I'm sure I don't look holy, and if you sat inside my head for very long, you'd have to take note of some remarkably unholy—alas, sometimes unkind—thoughts. I fail. I get up and try again, and blunder. And try again. I somehow believe there's goodness in the trying. After all, as I've said before, prayer is the only thing I can think of where "trying" is doing. Trying to pray is praying. God gets you, and you get to God.

I love the scenes in the Bible where Jesus calls the disciples to come follow him. Simon, also named Peter, and his brother, Andrew, were fishing, casting their nets into the sea, when Jesus walks by and says, "Follow me and I will make you fish for people," or "fishers of men," as we used to say. Wouldn't you wonder what Jesus meant by that? It's hard enough to catch fish in the sea of Galilee, but what would it mean to fish for people? I picture a hook with some bait on it, but these good folk use nets, far more efficient if not more demanding. What kind of net would it take to catch people? You could easily end up getting tangled among them.

Clearly Jesus was hugely alluring. With no apparent promises of reward, they left their work to follow him. How would they feed their families, let alone feed themselves, following this man? And what would the work entail? Today when we say "I'm a Jesus follower," it inevitably sounds like a bevy of spiritual commitments and ambitions. "You must be a believer," someone will tell me, suspecting some hidden or not-so-hidden sense of godliness in me. What if it could mean something simpler than that? When Jesus calls those people to follow him, I think it means to accompany him. To be present where he is present. To be in his orbit. To listen, watch, hear, and see. Will they be transformed? Yes, indeed. Follow me and I will make you fishers of people.

First, just follow.

Simon-Peter is the one I find easiest to identify with, at least in the Gospels. He gets it wrong again and again. He struggles to do the right thing. But early on, he sees it. His mother-in-law is sick with a high fever, and the followers ask Jesus about it. Jesus stands over the woman and "rebuke[s] the fever" as it says in Luke, and it leaves her.

I'm tempted to wonder if that's all that women were good for in the biblical era, to cook up a meal and serve the men. Was that why Jesus healed her? And "mother-in-law," it says. What about her daughter, Peter's wife? We never meet a spouse or hear about any offspring. Perhaps he was a widower, all the easier to pick up and go, but from the start the Bible makes clear that he has family. They need to be taken care of. His mother-in-law must be healed and is; it's one of the first things Jesus does. Wouldn't that be reason enough to follow him?

These fishermen leave behind their nets, but they don't leave their fishing profession behind, at least not initially. In the Gospel of John, after the Resurrection, when the disciples had already seen the risen Lord, showing himself to them, they once again can be found at sea. Jesus appears to them on the beach. They didn't know who he was at first (how hard it must have been to comprehend the unfathomable). They hadn't caught any fish yet, so he gave them instructions to cast their net on the right side. What a difference it makes. Peter's eyes are open. He is no longer Simon anyway. He has been renamed Peter by Jesus, which meant "rock" in the Greek, a bedrock for the faith of the church. He learns it's Jesus, and in a fit of enthusiasm, he jumps into the sea and swims toward him (these fishermen knew what the water was like). Jesus tells them to bring in the fish they had caught. There were 153 fish, a number so precise you can imagine them doing the counting, and yet the net was not torn. Why not accompany Jesus, even now?

Then, they must have remembered the first time Jesus got in a boat with them and told them where to cast their nets. That time the nets came close to breaking. According to the Gospel of Luke it seemed to have happened not long after Jesus healed Simon's mother-in-law. People were crowding around Jesus near the lake when he saw the fishermen's two boats. He got in Simon-Peter's boat and asked him to go a little way out from the shore, so Jesus could use it as he preached to the crowd.

There's no mention of any impatience on the part of the fishermen. But then they had worked all night and had caught nothing. Jesus the teacher and preacher becomes their work advisor, their coach. He tells them to head out into the deep water and let down their nets. Simon recounts the bad luck they've had so far, but dutifully they do as they are told. And they found great success, reeling in the nets. Both boats became so full they began to sink. Still in the boat, Simon-Peter fell to his knees before Jesus. "Go away from me, Lord, for I am a sinful man." Already he calls him "Lord." In this account, that's when Jesus says, "From now on, you will be catching people," filling their nets with needy souls.

How on earth to do that? Just hang out with Jesus. There's no book he makes them read, no papers to sign, no demanding confession. Just be present and listen. Miracles will happen. Later, in another account, when Peter sees Jesus approaching their boat, walking on water, he asks Jesus—if it really is Jesus—to command him to follow. "Come," Jesus says, just that one word, "Come." Peter steps out of the boat in faith and he does walk on water, at least for a little while. Then he notices the strong wind and his fears catch up with him. He begins to sink—as with most of us when our fears overwhelm us, sending us flailing. Peter cries out to be saved and Jesus extends a hand and catches him. "You of little faith, why did you doubt?" Jesus asks Peter. Why do we let doubts take over and rob us of our faith? The doubts might always be there, but they don't need to consume us or sink us.

There is also the extraordinary incident of the Transfiguration, when Jesus's identity was mystically revealed. He takes only three disciples with him to the mountain, where he prays and is illumined. His face shines like the sun and his humble clothes become a dazzling white, and Moses and Elijah appear, talking to him. Only the three, Peter, James, and John, are there to witness it. Peter wants to make three dwellings or booths for Jesus and the two prophets who are with him. He wants to mark the spot with something tangible. Instead, they get the message in a voice from heaven: "This is my Son, the Beloved." They fall to the ground in awe and fear.

The very human Jesus returns, telling them not to be afraid, and then on their way down the mountain, he insists they should tell no one of the vision until "after the Son of Man has been raised from the dead." It must have been impossible to grasp or understand. How could they share it when they didn't know what it meant?

At the Last Supper, Jesus wants to wash their feet. Peter doesn't want any part of it. Why should Jesus, his Lord, humiliate himself like that? Never. No way. Then again, when Jesus insists, Peter rushes headlong to be washed. "Lord, not my feet only but also my hands and my head." That fervor and devotion makes him so likeable. And yet, that same momentous night, when he is told by Jesus that he would be a deserter and deny knowing Jesus three times before the cock crows, he vehemently disagrees. Alas, he does just that, feeling the pain of it.

In the book of Acts, we meet a different Peter, a man of wisdom and unswerving faith, willing to suffer. In the Gospels, we see the journey he made to get there, an inner struggle even as he never gave up.

Jesus is not on hand waiting to issue report cards for his followers. He knows well enough the fears that face them, and the suffering that they'll endure. There's a foreshadowing of what it will take when he says, "Whoever does not take up the cross and follow me is not worthy of me." The cross, that instrument of torture and death, is like saying "take up the electric chair." It's all about letting go of those things you think define you, that seeming comfort zone. Those who find their life will lose it, and those who lose their life for Jesus's sake will find it. It's part of the journey, walking in the light, being in Jesus's presence.

"Whoever follows me will not walk in darkness," Jesus said, "but will have the light of life." What an invitation.

REFLECTIONS FOR MODERN LIVING

- Where do you look for Jesus?
- Do you hang out with people who are inspiring, helpful, thoughtful, compassionate?

25

YOU ARE THE LIGHT OF THE WORLD

Me? Not me. How can that be?

I'm always quicker to remember what Jesus says in the Gospel of John: "I am the light of the world. Whoever follows me will never walk in darkness but will have the light of life." Okay, Jesus, I got that. You are the light of the world. That makes sense.

But then I remember how, earlier in the Bible, in the Gospel of Matthew, we read Jesus saying something else: "You are the light of the world." *We* are. I believe that's an important pairing to live by—Jesus as the light, and Jesus calling us to shine as well.

We were put here—you were put here—to help light up the darkness. And the only way that can happen is if we let ourselves shine. That doesn't mean denying the darkness. We've already talked, however briefly, about the shadow self—the darkness we carry. That word, "shadow." Think about it: You don't really see a shadow until light is present. It's the light that makes the shadow visible. Like those shadow puppets that fascinated me as a kid—the figures were tiny, but the shadows on the wall loomed, immense.

Jesus is indeed the light of the world. That's what this little writing project is meant to illuminate—to help you see Jesus, and to help me see and follow him. The world is dark and dangerous, yes, but not when Jesus is beside us or before us. He is a beacon—a floodlight that reveals life's potholes, pitfalls, and hidden beauty.

"Thank you, Jesus. I saw that . . . and wouldn't have seen it without your help."

And at the same time, we too are meant to be lights.

Think of how often we use "light" as a verb: His face lit up. She lit up the room. She lit me on fire. We're not just glowing by reflected light. We carry it within us. We're not simply moons to God's sun. We are made to shine with God's goodness, compassion, love, and mercy. And here's the beautiful twist—light doesn't diminish when shared. It multiplies.

"Jesus Christ, have mercy on me"—that's a prayer I say countless times. Sometimes the longer version: "Lord Jesus Christ, Son of God, have mercy on me, a sinner." Call it a mantra, if you like. Cross out "sinner" if it trips you up—but for me, it puts things in the right order. I am nothing more, and nothing less, than a lowly sinner.

And from that low place, I can shine. I can bend down to help. I can be the glow that helps someone else light up.

We need time alone to recharge our light. Jesus did. He withdrew from crowds to pray. We need to do the same—checking out to check in.

The onslaught of news, noise, and algorithms is always there to distract us. Fear is easy to monetize. The headlines keep us clicking but rarely give us light.

The glow of your phone isn't always the glow of the Lord. You'll know by what you're looking at.

That's why I close my eyes to pray now. It used to puzzle me—why close your eyes? But now it's my go-to. With eyes shut, I can better see the light that shines. I picture it in my mind's eye. I imagine God's light glowing there.

Jesus says no one lights a lamp and hides it under a basket. You put it on a stand. So it can illuminate the house—and the people inside it. "Let your light shine before others," he says, "so that they may see your good works and give glory to your Father in heaven."

There's that quote, often attributed to St. Francis of Assisi: "Preach the Gospel at all times. If necessary, use words." Whether or not he said it, he surely lived it.

Francis showed his love through actions. Assisi, his hometown, remains a place where heaven seems to kiss the earth. He was a light for the world not by preaching with a bullhorn, but by how he lived.

Would that I had an ounce of that. Would that any of us did.

So how do we shine? By doing good. By listening to that inner tug—send that note, make that call, offer that seat, hold that silence, forgive that grudge—and answering it.

Let your prayer closet illuminate your daily walk. Recharge there so you're ready to shine out here.

"This little light of mine, I'm going to let it shine . . ." We sang it in Sunday school. I sing it now with our soup kitchen guests at church. So simple. So fun. So holy. Letting people sing together—there's light in that. Harmony itself is a form of courage.

You are the light of the world. Don't be afraid to shine.

Reflections for Modern Living

- What makes your light shine? What ignites it?
- Who are the people in your life who shine on you?
- Do you ever turn to worship music or Scripture to find and share the light?
- If we are meant to be light, where do you let yours shine?

26

GET RID OF WHAT GETS IN THE WAY

Ever feel yourself going down some endless rabbit hole of anger, lust, fantasies of revenge, hate?

It can be so easy. That colleague who made those outrageous allegations, so full of themself, has made, you suspect, more than a few nasty comments about you behind your back. Just that phrase "behind your back" says so much—it implies that someone is sneaking around. Surely you could pay them back by pointing out their alleged misbehavior to a few sympathetic ears, getting the others on your side. You versus them, or better yet, us versus them. They'll roast for sure. A few bad comments and talks with the boss, and they'll be on the exit ramp, thanks to you.

Think about all the energy that took, all the distractions, the strategizing, research even; it might have gotten in the way of you doing your own job to the best of your ability. You could have told yourself that you were doing it for the good of the company or others, getting rid of excess baggage, but think about it: Were you really letting your light shine? Or was it more like trying to turn off some other light? Where was goodness? Where was faith? Where was love?

Jesus is looking for transparency, and that's hard to have when you're deep into manipulation. The darndest thing about manipulation is that you often don't even know you're at it. Criticism can be painful. I must force myself to welcome it because it is sure to tell me something about myself, even if I adamantly disagree. In fact, the more I disagree, the more there might be to learn. Feeling uncomfortable could be just the thing.

The word "sin" can sound so high-minded and theological that we forget it's real. It has always amused me that the phrase "living in sin" has become a sexual reference, as though that's all that sin is about or that that's the worst sort of sin we could possibly commit. What about pride, anger, hatred, blame, selfishness, dishonesty, arrogance, gluttony, laziness, envy, greed? So much in our culture is calculated to appeal to those dark sides of our nature. Think (again) of the ads on our screens, lavish images speaking to our greed, boosting it while barely acknowledging some hidden agenda.

In fact, the hiddenness of sin is part of sin's doings. You envy that gorgeous owner of a new car or new suit. You long for that tropical vacation or world cruise that would seemingly relieve you of all your worries in one fell swoop. The envy has blurred the lines of good sense. "Oh, if I only had the money . . ." you start thinking. "Maybe if I charged it on my credit card and then put a few bucks in the lottery. You never know." *You never know.* It's as though the thing itself will rid you of any negative feelings.

Cut it out, Jesus says, and he goes whole hog in such an outrageous statement that it's worth quoting in full. "If your right eye causes you to sin, tear it out and throw it away; it is better for you to lose one of your members than for your whole body to be thrown into hell. And if your right hand causes you to sin, cut it off and throw it away; it is better for you to lose one of your members than for your whole body to go into hell."

Yikes, Jesus. Are we really supposed to dismember ourselves? I don't think so, but he knows a powerful statement will get our attention. Just when you want to turn the page and go to something sweeter, he's caught you. How are you going to put the disturbing passage out of your mind? *Cut it off.* Cut what off? Even just taking it metaphorically, you're going to have to look at what gets in the way of you leading a rich, rewarding life of faith.

Are those pretty pictures in the TV ad just there to amuse you or are they asking more? How do you respond? What part of your nature is being addressed? Is that politician really appealing to the better part of your nature or are they working at getting your vote by making you mad as hell? Sure, there can be truth in what they're saying, but are you aware of how they're reaching you? Is there something in what they're saying that will make you love your neighbor as yourself or, harder still, love your enemies?

Sometimes by acting externally you can hit what's messing you up internally. You can cut it out. Change the channels. Push the off button. Delete that email even before you read it. Put your phone away for a while. And do something good with the time you've saved. Do something outrageous.

I'm sitting on a trans-continental flight next to a woman with a fifteen-month-old baby squirming in her lap. The kid keeps kicking me. I want to be outraged. Someone needs to pay attention to *me*. After all the miles I've racked up with this airline, don't I deserve better? I figured I could buzz the flight attendant and request a different seat. Wasn't there some room up there in first class? I should earn some extra miles for my endless patience. Rewards. Just that word, the way it's used as a marketing technique. Rewards, something we deserve, like a front-row seat in heaven. But wait a minute . . . isn't there something far more duplicitous going on inside?

I need to take a minute to notice where my self-importance is taking me. The baby is incredibly cute, and the mom endlessly patient. When the flight attendant comes by to sell headphones for the TV, the mom wants a pair, but alas, all she has is cash. The transaction can only be done with a credit card. *Do something, Rick.* "I can pay for it," I say, pulling out my card. "I can give you the cash," she says. *Cut it out.* It's only six bucks, and I get a 50 percent discount. Greed would take me to hell. I might even get an extra three bucks out of my fake generosity. "No need," I say to the woman.

Don't get too wigged out by Jesus's use of the word "hell" here. My study Bible says it's probably a reference to Gehenna, a hellish garbage-strewn spot in the Holy Land, not nice by any means, even if it's not exactly the torturous place Dante describes in his *Inferno.* The next time that little baby kicked up her little feet and put them in my lap, I was touched. "I'm sorry," said the mom. "Don't worry," I said. There was a bit of heaven next to me to be experienced, but only when I cut something else out.

What's getting in between you and God? There can be all sorts of things and a culture that will help you justify your worst behavior. Less can be more. Let God help you find the things you need to cut out.

REFLECTIONS FOR MODERN LIVING

- What are the biggest distractions for you—the things that get in the way of your spiritual life?
- Could you draw up a list of your least favorite qualities and what sparks them?
- When have you felt most loved by God?
- Have you ever experienced the power of writing down the things you're most grateful for, day after day?

27

THE PAIN DOESN'T LAST FOREVER

There's an old story about a woman who goes to church on Easter Monday, and as she's leaving, she pauses to chat with an aged, disheveled woman selling corsages and boutonnieres on the front steps. Despite her impoverished appearance, the lady is full of smiles.

"How is that possible?" wonders the woman coming out of the church, and they talk for a while.

Yes, indeed, the old woman has experienced suffering, but she takes comfort in the message of Easter. It's a truth she has known first-hand. The pain and horror of Good Friday were turned into the power and mystery of the Resurrection. It's "the magic of three days," as she describes it. Pain inevitably comes in our lives, but as Jesus taught and experienced, it doesn't last forever. He even compares it to what a woman goes through in giving birth to a child. "When a woman is in labor, she has pain. . . . But when her child is born, she no longer remembers the anguish because of the joy of having brought a human being into the world," he says in the Gospel of John. The misery and anguish are overpowered by the joy of that newborn child.

As a father of two, I witnessed my wife go through the agony of labor and then the joy of holding a little boy in her arms. Of course, as a guy, I couldn't begin to say how that bliss could make the misery forgettable, and I want to say, "Jesus, you're a guy here . . . are you really sure?"

Of course, he was using a metaphor to prepare the disciples for what would happen in the coming days, the tragedy of the Crucifixion—and part of the tragedy was seeing most of his own beloved followers abandon him—followed by the miracle of the Resurrection.

"So you have pain now," Jesus says, "but I will see you again, and your hearts will rejoice, and no one will take your joy from you." *Pain now* . . . how could they have had any idea of what was to come, no matter how many hints Jesus had given them? Then again, in our lives here on earth, there is no telling for sure what the future will bring. I find myself invariably entertained—if not irritated—by the predictions the wisest, best-trained economists make about the future, and just how things turn out. Some are right, some are wrong, but who has the perfect crystal ball? Jesus, for sure, even when there are moments when he is perfectly human and therefore uncertain, or perhaps he simply prefers to leave it unsaid, like when he said about his second coming, "But about that day or hour no one knows, neither the angels in heaven, nor the Son, but only the Father." Leave it up to God.

When we experience pain, it can feel like it will go on forever. "Will I ever get out of this mess?" we ask ourselves. Will life go back to what it was before? Is there no hope?

There is *always* hope. That's what Jesus is telling us. And in any painful situation, we need to hold on to that. I remember noting a therapist, counseling a patient who had used the word "never." The patient said flat out that things would *never* change and only get worse. The therapist said, "Don't use that word 'never.'"

What we can't ever do (see, I'm trying to avoid using the word "never") is put blinders on when we're in pain. I'm not crazy about that slogan used in gyms, "No pain, no gain." It's as though we're simply supposed to grit our teeth and get through the worst. Grunt and groan as you lift those weights or run on the treadmill because soon enough it'll be over. The French have the expression, "*Il faut souffrir pour être belle*," claiming that beauty comes through suffering.

Still, pain—it's not fun to admit—can be a necessary teacher. That can only happen if we *allow* it to teach us. There are stages of this. Go ahead and have that conversation with God to complain, "Stop it. I don't want this. Rid me of it." Beneath all that anger there might be some real fear to confront, and how can you confront it if you haven't dealt with the anger? *What is this about, God? What am I supposed to learn here?*

May God bless those friends and loved ones who sit or walk with us on the journey, who listen, who comfort, who—when we're ready to hear—offer insights. I've had times when I've really messed up as a father, as a spouse. I would give credit to my wife that our marriage has thrived as it has, and also to our faith community. There is something enormously powerful about sitting in the intimacy of a church service Sunday after Sunday, praying together, listening to a sermon, hearing Scripture. You find your way to shared understanding and emotional growth, even without talking about it. And yes, there have been those times we needed to reach out to a professional counselor or therapist, a trained and sympathetic ear.

I've also already mentioned the help I've found in the workplace when I failed, when I messed up, when I needed help, when I found advice. Again and again—how did my dear colleagues put up with it?—I was given a chance to grow, and did, God love them.

When you go through those trying times, it's essential to know that the trials will not last forever. Joy comes in the morning, as the Psalmist famously said. And in the evening and midday and at night too. The trials the disciples went through were meant to prepare them for the even greater trials they would face. Be that person. The pain will not last forever.

This isn't going to sound like much, but it's example of pain—tooth pain, to be exact—and its amazingly quick resolution. Worries crowding my head, none exactly dental, I was finishing my breakfast when, yikes, I bit something hard. I spit it out. A piece of a tooth. I called my dentist's office immediately. It was a Thursday, and they're not open on Friday, let alone the weekend. I hoped I could see the dentist that day. The assistant answered the phone, looked up my file, asked if I could come in that very morning at 9:30. I checked the time on my phone. It was 8:45. With luck, I could get to the dentist's office in forty-five minutes, but I'd have to dart out immediately, without even changing out of my running clothes or brushing my teeth. "Sure," I said, leaving the rest in the good Lord's hands.

I put on my raincoat—it was spitting outside—dashed out, got on the A train, changed trains at 42nd Street, got out on Madison Avenue, right across the street from the good dentist's office. I walked in the building, dug into my pocket to find my driver's license—picture ID was requested—and showed it to the man at the downstairs security desk. Just as he was looking at it, a young woman passed by and said, "Frederick." *Frederick?* That's *my* full name. "Is that your name?" I asked the security guy. "No," he said. "She just likes to call me by a different name every day. Today it's Frederick." What a hoot.

I followed the young woman into the elevator and told her, "You know, my name is Frederick." "Oh," she said. We laughed. I got out on the thirteenth floor. Turned out to be the wrong floor. Went back down and asked the guy at the security desk which floor for my beloved dentist. "Twelfth," he said. It was 9:31 when I walked into the office. I was shown a room and a chair to sit in. Yes, a chipped tooth.

"We could do a crown," the dentist said, "but that's awfully expensive. Let's try just putting the chip back on." And he did, with glue. (The good dentist is not one who always goes for the most expensive option, truly a trustworthy guy.)

He finished up in half an hour. I paused at the assistant's desk. Pay now or later? "Later," she said. "Let's first see how much your insurance will cover." "Great," I said. Often enough the biggest pain I deal with at the dentist's office is in the back pocket, where the wallet sits, but let's face it, there's a huge element of privilege here. That I have a dentist who is so easy to get in touch with, that he trusts me to pay whatever the fee will be, that something can be fixed that quickly, that I can trust him as much as I trust God, perhaps even more, is a blessing I don't take for granted.

I got back on the subway and arrived home a little before 11:00. The pain didn't last long. And there was some joy in the whole thing. Savor that, Frederick. At least until the bill comes.

Reflections for Modern Living

- Have you ever experienced the turnaround "magic of three days"?
- How do you hold on to hope when a situation feels hopeless?
- Can you express your anger to God, knowing that God understands?
- Can there be a spiritual blessing to be found in the midst of chronic pain?

28

JUDGE NOT

A fellow choir member, a woman who was an attorney and then became a judge, said that her new job changed her time in church. She could hear Jesus's command, "Judge not, and you will not be judged . . ." with different ears and new insight. She'd tell herself that she was expected to judge—it was her professional duty. All the more reason not to do it when it *wasn't* her job, when it *wasn't* her calling. And that could be challenging. For her and for all of us.

I've already hinted at this—how judgmental I can be. There will be a little voice going on in my head—and it's not a recording—saying things like, "Gosh, she's really been putting on the weight lately" or "Why isn't he looking for a new job? He's always complaining about the one he's got" or "I can't believe they're spending all that money on an interior decorator when they can barely afford the second mortgage they took out on their home" or "No wonder their kids are getting in trouble. They never disciplined them enough or even gave them a curfew." On and on it goes. What you might notice is that it's always about other people. Why not look at myself?

That can be very hard. We can be terribly blind about our own faults, especially when we expend so much energy and

time looking for and at the so-called faults of others. Didn't Jesus say, with memorably playful imagery, "Why do you see the speck in your neighbor's eye, but do not notice the log in your own eye?" Doesn't that log get in your way? You might even go a step further and say to your neighbor or friend, "Let me take that speck out of your eye," all the while ignoring your own blind spots. Seems to me this can be even worse in our digital age, with algorithms sending us news and updates that coalesce with our own views. We log on and never see the logs.

One of the crucial mental and spiritual practices is to give yourself some quiet, meditative, prayerful time. I do so every morning for half an hour, as I've mentioned, sitting on our lumpy sofa. In busier, more hectic days I did it on my commute to work, giving me the title of one of my first books about prayer, *Finding God on the A Train* (and a source of amusement when someone calls it "finding God on the/a train"). It might sound like a blissful, peace-filled spiritual rendezvous with God, but I've got to admit—at least for me—it's also a time for self-investigation and discovery. I'll be sitting there in prayer, focusing on the good Lord, and sure enough, some niggling issue will interrupt my holy thoughts.

I can't believe what that guy said in that meeting. I'm so much smarter than he is and have a lot more to contribute. He's so oblivious and rambles on and on. . . .

Wait. Might that be me too? How might I appear to the other guy? Call me oblivious and self-assured. Who is judging whom? Worries about money and finances inevitably creep into the holy time. Do I trust in God to provide? Do I think of Jesus's message about the birds of the air or lilies of the field? Or what about when I start cogitating about my health? Doesn't this time remind me to look for God's health, to remember how crucial my spirituality is to my well-being? Instead, I can be guilty of making comparisons, like "I sure do eat better than that guy chomping on that burger and fries" or "At least I get more exercise than so-and-so. No wonder she's having trouble with her back. If she only did some of the healthy stretching that *I* do."

I would say that these distractions during my spiritual time are also one of the benefits of it. In the context of a "God moment," I'm forced to see how I fail, how faulty I am, how judgmental. You can't really "judge not" till you realize you are judging, and that sort of self-honesty isn't always easy to come by. In fact, there's a lot out there urging us to ignore our faults, asking us to focus on the failings of others.

I'll circle back again to what sometimes comes up in our news sources, how we can be asked to see how "wrong" the other guy is. Yes, perhaps they are, but where is that telling paragraph that explains how maybe they aren't . . . or did I find myself skipping that part of the story? Is it possible that I do the same with people that come into my life? Why not look for the things that might motivate them, the suffering they might have endured, the reasons for why I'm so quick to judge? Again and again, Jesus points out that the enriching spiritual place is to be with those who bemoan their sinful state. You can't change until you're willing to admit how wrong you are or how you're struggling to get something right—if you could only see it right. *Judge not and you will not be judged.*

"Do not condemn, and you will not be condemned," Jesus says in the Gospel of Luke. What rich territory you can enter. "Forgive, and you will be forgiven." Of course, that's not easy, but look what comes down the pike. "Give, and it will be given to you. A good measure, pressed down, shaken together, running over, will be put into your lap; for the measure you give will be the measure you get back." Quid pro quo, *pressed down, shaken together, running over* . . . It sounds like the recipe for a delicious smoothie.

To forgive someone can feel so wrong. Don't they realize what they've done? Don't they see how they've hurt me and others? But holding onto that act, that dark moment, that pernicious behavior, that terrible memory, can be dangerous to the soul. Would that I could "let it go"—to sing that Disney song from *Frozen*. Would that I could move on. Some sort of spiritual/moral accounting needs to take place. I can only do that with God's help.

My father and his younger brother had a falling out many years ago. For a while we didn't see our uncle and aunt or our beloved cousins. I never understood what had happened—and didn't learn much about it till much later—but it felt sad, both for us and for Dad. What I do remember is how wonderful it was when things were patched up, the sheer delight and joy of it. What Dad and his brother did at that time was also to decide to forget what had divided them. There was no inventory of what had gone wrong. No accusations made. They simply started anew with a blank slate, and the love that had always been there came tumbling back.

To forgive and forget, to really do that, someone has to forgive first. In the Lord's Prayer we say, "Forgive us our debts as we forgive our debtors" or "Forgive us our trespasses as we forgive those who trespass against us" or "Forgive us our sins as we forgive those who sin against us." No matter which version you use, notice the tit for tat. We forgive as we are forgiven. That means acknowledging the wrongs you have committed. That means confronting your judgmental self as you come to see how flawed you really are. I recall—with a smile—how Mom would try to open us up to this side of our nature (as she acknowledged it in herself). "I can't believe how mean that kid at school is," we might complain. "I'm sorry," she would say. "He must not be very happy."

Start seeing others as you come to see yourself.

REFLECTIONS FOR MODERN LIVING

- Can you hear yourself being judgmental?
- What criteria fosters your greatest criticism—intellectual ability, physical appearance, spirituality, emotional intelligence?
- Where do you see people being particularly quick in their judgments?
- Is judgmental behavior on your part ever a reflection of your own insecurities?

29

MOVE FOREVER FORWARD

Another anecdote about Mom: Shortly before her death, at age ninety-three, we were chatting on the phone. She lived thousands of miles away, on the other coast, and I made a habit of calling her every Sunday, just to check in. This Sunday she was worried about something within her, something that went back to her childhood, something she didn't like and still couldn't get rid of: the antisemitism she'd grown up with.

"I just don't like it," she said. "I want to get rid of it. I need to keep working on that."

She'd grown up in a WASP suburb that was still mostly WASP in my childhood when we lived there. Things have changed over the years. It isn't as lily white as it had been, but in its homogenous days, prejudices would flourish without being challenged. If you didn't run into someone from another faith background or different ethnicity, you didn't have to look too carefully at your knee-jerk reflections. I remember going off to college and being intrigued to discover how many of my classmates were Jewish. When I mentioned that to Mom, back in the day, she said, "Oh . . . they're very smart." And then she referred to her experience as a docent, giving tours at LA County Art Museum across town. "Many of the other docents are Jewish."

The way she said it: they were other—or maybe Other—and so they remained. Over the years, she might have had more interactions with Jewish friends or friends of friends and then in-laws of my brother-in-law (her son-in-law), wonderful, delightful people. She'd been with them many a time. That Sunday evening when we spoke, she'd been at a family celebration where they had been included. She'd enjoyed their company. And yet, she noticed something unattractive still going on inside, a visceral reaction that she wanted to get rid of.

"It's just inside of me, and I don't like it," she'd said, prejudices that were fed, I suspect, by long-ago conversations with her father or cryptic remarks her own mother had made ("I love my mother," she would say, "but I don't always like her").

And here she was, at ninety-three, trying to do something about it.

Recently we've seen some monstrous incidents of antisemitism. At the time my conversation with Mom spoke movingly to me about something I would aspire to do at any age, to work at changing myself. To seek to grow. To move forward. To know of the danger that would come if I didn't. No looking back here, even at that age, if change were to be made. Spiritual growth, emotional growth, the changes that can come of it, need to be embraced every step of the way. Maybe we don't become whole in our earthly lives, achieving our goals, but we must push to reach forward all the way.

I've always been a big fan of the forementioned *Divine Comedy* by the great Italian poet Dante Alighieri, that vivid poetic description of the afterlife, from hell to purgatory to heaven. Of the three books my favorite is the middle one: *Il Purgatorio.* The notion of purgatory is not necessarily something I subscribe to doctrinally, but it speaks to me as a metaphor for change and growth. Growing up in a Protestant denomination, I'd never heard of it. Not till I went off to college and studied the literature of different eras and cultures, finally reading *The Divine Comedy*—a comedy not because it offered some bucketful of laughs but because it told a transformative saga with a happy ending.

What fascinated me about Dante's vision of the afterlife is that if you had the good fortune to arrive in the middle zone, purgatory, all the work you had started on earth, the baby steps of spiritual growth, would be continued. You'd keep climbing to heaven. What mattered most was that you made a start, heading in the right direction. To be a little bit like my mom, to rid myself of the stuff that got in the way of being wholly loving and faith filled.

Jesus, fully human as he was divine, understood this so well. You can hear his impatience with his listeners. It's as though he might have shouted it at times. "No one who puts a hand to the plow and looks back is fit for the kingdom of God," he says. If you look back while plowing, you're not going to make a straight line. You'll swerve off course.

The Lord's admonition comes when a potential follower makes excuses. "First let me go and bury my father," he says, a worthy, necessary duty for any son. The question is: Has the father died just recently or have the rituals not been made yet? If this would-be follower was out and about, able to address Jesus, he probably *has* done all the necessary work of mourning prescribed by his faith (an insight coming to me from scholar and teacher Geza Vermes's book *The Authentic Gospel of Jesus*). Jesus's impatience is obvious. He knows an excuse when he hears one. Maybe it makes his answer seem less shocking. "Let the dead bury their own dead," he says, "but as for you, go and proclaim the kingdom of God."

We are so good at making excuses. They litter the holy ground we walk upon, ready to trip us up lest we be aware of them. You can't pay full attention to the task at hand if you're distracted looking back. Look forward and lean forward. The worries when they're slain can bury their own dead.

REFLECTIONS FOR MODERN LIVING

- What would you most like to change about yourself?
- How can you use prayer to grow in faith?
- What most tempts you to look back instead of moving forward?
- Do you ever turn to your faith community, a family member, or a good friend to help you change?

30

Make it a Secret

More than once, we read in the Gospels how Jesus performed a healing or brought someone back to life, and then, oddly enough, urged those present to "Tell no one." For instance, when the leper came to him, knelt, and said, "If you choose, you can make me clean." Jesus did just that, saying, "I do choose. Be made clean!"

I do choose. Bingo. But then Jesus said to the man, "See that you say nothing to anyone." Well, not just anyone in this case. "Go, show yourself to the priest," Jesus went on, "and offer the gift that Moses commanded, as a testimony to them." *To them.* At least the powers that be were supposed to know. But that would be enough. No one else was supposed to know.

Take another incident, when he healed two blind men. He asked first if they believed he could even do such a thing. "Yes, Lord," they dutifully replied. They believed. Then he touched their eyes, proclaiming, "According to your faith let it be done to you." Their eyes were miraculously opened. Was Jesus's touch really needed if their faith was what healed them? Here he touched, but often there's not even that.

After such an amazing experience, wouldn't you want to shout out to the world? How would *you* respond to hearing Jesus's injunction, "See that no one knows." No one?

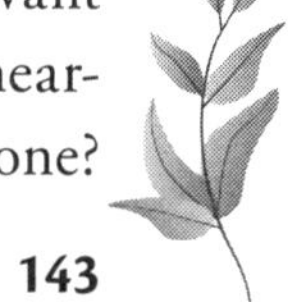

Really, Lord? In this instance, they disobeyed and went around their neighborhood, spreading the good news. Thrilled to have their vision returned, they wanted to show it and share it.

Or when he visited the girl who had died. Once again, he encouraged those who came to him to believe something other than what they had seen with their own eyes. "Only believe, and she will be saved." But, when he went inside, there was more weeping and wailing.

"Do not weep," Jesus said, "for she is not dead but sleeping." Could they see her chest rising and falling with every new breath? Hardly, it seems. They laughed at him, knowing that she was dead. Here, again, he offered his touch, taking her by the hand and calling out, "Child, get up!" The spirit returned to her and she got up at once. He instructed them to give her something to eat—Jesus could be very practical. Then he told her astounded parents to tell no one what happened.

Somebody must have said something, given their testimony, or would the story have even landed in the Gospels? Some wise souls have explained that in instances like these, Jesus was trying to keep people focused on the bigger message of why he had come to earth. It wasn't just to be a healer of the body, but he was also here to heal the soul. He had to address big issues like justice and peace and the transformation of the world and didn't want his followers to get sidetracked by all these happy stories of healing and restoration. They would see him as *a* savior without the "the" attached to it or an uppercase "S."

I also think he wanted those who experienced his miracles to hold them deep inside, to ponder them, to rejoice in them, to reflect on them, to let their minds embrace the big change.

If they just went around telling people, it could lose some of its power.

One of the liveliest stories of a blind man's healing—referred to a bit earlier—lies in the Gospel of John when Jesus and his disciples came upon a man who was blind from birth, and the disciples asked Jesus who had sinned to cause this blindness. We might think, "Goodness, how unfair to blame the blindness on some person, on some personal failing." And yet, doesn't that often lurk in our minds? You want to blame someone for their suffering. If they only had a better diet and didn't eat all that awful ultra-processed food, not to mention the exercise they don't seem to get. Sure, diet and exercise are important, but they can't explain everything. (Just ask this slim, seemingly healthy runner why he's ended up in the hospital too many times.)

In this case Jesus tells the disciples that the man was born blind "so that God's works might be revealed in him," so that Jesus can perform a miracle, so that he can do the good work he has come to earth to do. "As long as I am in the world, I am the light of the world," he says. Then he spits on the ground, makes some mud and spreads it on the man's eyes and instructs him to wash in "the pool of Siloam." The man did so and could see, thanks to the healing mud of Jesus.

Jesus gave him no specific instructions on keeping silent, but the world wouldn't let him shut up. Some wondered if he was even the same man, the same blind beggar. He kept insisting, "Yes, I am." Well, how had it all happened? He went on to be his own witness, "The man called Jesus made mud, spread it on my eyes, and said to me, 'Go to Siloam and wash.'" Some wondered, where was this Jesus? Why didn't he stick around to claim credit for what he had done? Turned out the whole thing happened on the Sabbath, which gave the Pharisees more ammunition for criticism. No work should be done on the Sabbath, and hadn't Jesus done some real work, concocting a potion of spit and mud?

The parents are trotted out for their testimony. Yes, they say, their son had been born blind, but they don't want to call any attention to the miracle maker or give Jesus credit, lest they be attacked by the Pharisees. See what happens when the word gets spread. See how something even as good as healing a beggar's blindness gets twisted around. No one wants to give God the glory, nor his Son. The changed man says, with some exasperation, "One thing I know, that though I was blind, now I see." *Though I was blind, now I see.* The words have a metaphorical ring to them for all of us. However ignorant we have been, narrow in our thinking and blind to our own faults, Jesus comes around to wipe the darkness from our eyes. Now we can see.

The healed man gets it, despite the attacks. "If this man were not from God," he says to the disclaimers, "he could do nothing." His listeners refuse to go with it. How hard it can be to accept a miracle, especially one that has happened to someone you want to blame for their misfortune. The man is driven out from their midst, and Jesus, in compassion, seeks him out. Now comes a bigger miracle. Go for the metaphor.

"Do you believe in the Son of Man?" Jesus asks. "Who is he, sir?" the man asks. Jesus tells him, shows him. "The one speaking with you is he," Jesus says. "Lord, I believe," the man says, as simple as that, worshipping the Lord. Jesus spins it around, going for the deeper healing and the tragedy of moral, spiritual blindness. "I have come into this world for judgment so that those who do not see may see, and those who do see may become blind."

Hold all that deep inside.

REFLECTIONS FOR MODERN LIVING

- Is there ever a danger of talking about faith rather than simply living it?
- Can silence speak more than words?
- Do you think Jesus would want each of us to share any miracles we've ever experienced on social media?
- Is there a temptation in our modern world to pin the blame on others for their misfortunes?

31

LOOK AT YOUR PREJUDICES

Carl Jung, the great psychiatrist, therapist, and teacher, has a theory that I've found very helpful: We're all born with both good and evil parts of us. We all have a dark side. Pay attention to it, be aware. Not for nothing do we confess our sins in our faith tradition and in the Lord's Prayer, whether you call them sins or debts or trespasses. The danger I've seen, and have been guilty of myself, as I've mentioned, is to project that shadow self on others instead of confronting it in myself.

In any social situation, I find myself most irritated by guys—and it's always some guy—who talk too much, dominating the conversation. You know, guys who might be a lot like me. How much easier it is to dislike those qualities in someone else than to face up to them in myself.

Jesus understood and was especially attentive to the biases and prejudices of his own era. Again and again, clear-thinking prophets and teachers like Martin Luther King Jr. come along to help us see the truth. And yet, don't we need to work on this dark side of ourselves forever? I've mentioned that phone chat with my mom, not long before she died at age ninety-three, when she revealed how her unconscious—now made conscious—antisemitic bias bothered her.

"I want to get rid of it," she said. "I have to keep working at it." Keep working, even at that advanced age. Perhaps that's one reason she had lived so long. She was always working at it, and working at it, trying to improve herself.

Those things can only happen if we're willing to look to our dark sides and acknowledge them. Let me go to a story about Jesus that has baffled many. He had retreated into a house—to go with the version in the Gospel of Mark—and hoped that no one would notice he was there. Alas, he'd been followed by a woman, a Gentile, "of Syrophoenician origin," or we might say Greek. She kneels before him, bowing down at his feet. She'd heard about Jesus's healing power and desperately needs it for her daughter, who is plagued by some demon or unclean spirit. She begs for his help. Jesus almost sounds flippant when he responds, "Let the children be fed first," by which he means the children of Israel, his own people, not such foreigners like her. "For it is not fair to take the children's food and throw it to the dogs."

Wow, what a nasty thing to say, a line that seems impossible for such a holy man, God's own son, mind you. I've heard preachers say that this is just because Jesus is human. He, too, can be prejudiced like all of us. He doesn't want to heal the woman's daughter, not someone like her. But maybe he is simply testing the woman, to see how sincere she is. I think he's also testing his listeners. He knows their prejudices and is vividly mirroring them. To be called a dog in that era would have been an incalculable insult.

The woman is not turned off nor crushed by his words. "Sir," she comes back and says, "even the dogs under the table eat the children's crumbs." (I've often thought that's one advantage of having a dog; all those crumbs get eaten up to save you from having to sweep them up yourself!)

Jesus is touched by her faith and humility and does what she asks without even meeting the daughter. "For saying that," he says, "you may go—the demon has left your daughter." She goes home and finds that's true, the child lying in bed, the demon gone.

Did we just witness two sides of Jesus, the dark, biased human and the transcendent divine? I don't think so. Jesus is Jesus when he's here on earth, human and divine at once. He can mimic the prejudices of his people and use the occasion to show how they can be transcended. We need to do the same. Look to your biases. Look to those dark, prejudiced sides of yourself. Notice them even if it makes you miserably uncomfortable. You can't change until you see and acknowledge what needs to be changed. Notice that dark side of your nature so you can embrace the light.

You are the light of the world, and Jesus is too.

Reflections for Modern Living

- Do you have a regular practice of asking for God's forgiveness?
- Have you ever unwittingly revealed your own prejudices and/or biases in some email, text, or comment you made so quickly it didn't seem obvious?
- What does it mean to be truly open-minded?
- If you accept some darker part of yourself, does it become easier to accept it in others, and therefore easier to forgive and love?

32

LOSE YOURSELF TO FIND YOURSELF

I cling shamelessly to everything that matches up with who I think I am, or at least who I want people to think I am. Isn't social media just perfect for that? I can post the images that make me seem most attractive. See, I am all dressed up, going to some fancy party. Or look at me at that book signing, people lining up to get a copy of the latest with my signature on it. Perhaps I am giving a talk at some church, gesturing with one hand. It's all good for marketing. That's what you need to do, you know, to get people to buy a copy of your latest. Get them to click into Amazon, where they can read a few readers' reviews (many of them posted at your kindly urging, or rather their kindlier responding).

You'd found something to share. Why would anybody want to log on if you were lost? It's too scary to be lost.

And yet doesn't the greatest power for transformation often come to us when we're at the bottom, when we know we can't do it on our own anymore, when we desperately need to turn to God for help? I haven't suffered from alcoholism or drug addiction, but I have been continually inspired by people who have turned their lives around through devotion and rigorous

commitment to what they've learned and done in twelve-step groups. What I've heard and seen is that they need to bottom out before they can truly turn around, before they reach up and grow.

There is so much in those twelve steps, for anybody, and certainly for those of us who yearn to follow Jesus. "We admitted we were powerless over alcohol," reads the first of those twelve steps, "that our lives had become unmanageable." I can't begin to imagine how difficult that must be, to admit you can't do it on your own, to completely let go. And curiously enough, to let go to hold on to something greater.

"Whoever loves father or mother more than me is not worthy of me," Jesus says, "and whoever loves son or daughter more than me is not worthy of me; and whoever does not take up the cross and follow me is not worthy of me. Those who find their life will lose it, and those who lose their life for my sake will find it."

Of course, we love those beloved family members, but notice it's about priorities, loving them, loving anybody, loving even the life God has given us, more than we love God. We can better serve our loved ones by loving God first. We've talked already about the dangers of defining yourself by group identity. "I'm a member of this family," we might say, or "I'm a member of this team," or "I'm a member of this political party," or "I'm a member of this corporation," or even "I'm a member of this church." Is the church more important than the God we serve?

God wants us to be who we are, not who someone else *thinks* we might be. Our standards for behavior and being come from God, not from some litmus test designed and promulgated by others. Your parents and siblings might have some plan for you and about you that might seem admirable, but is it really you? Think how Jesus shocked his parents when he was just a boy. Every year, as we read in the Gospel of Luke, they would go to Jerusalem to celebrate the Passover. To get there from their home in Nazareth would be a trip, probably about a week's journey—obviously walking, not driving.

As I mentioned earlier, when Jesus was twelve, they went for the festival and then returned, but Jesus stayed behind. It took them a while to realize he was missing—they obviously trusted him (like our parents trusting us when we were old enough to run around the neighborhood playing with our friends, making sure we were home in time for dinner). After searching high and low in Jerusalem, they found him in the temple, listening to the teachers and asking them questions. They're shocked and disappointed, all this searching that delayed their safe journey home. Had they already forgotten the mystical things that had happened at his birth? Had Mary forgotten what the angel of the Lord had promised, inspiration for her glorious song, magnifying the Lord, "for he has looked with favor on the lowliness of his handmaiden"?

"Why were you searching for me?" the adolescent Jesus asked. "Did you not know that I must be in my Father's house?" *My Father's house?* No, they hadn't understood. No light bulb went off in their heads that reminded them, "Oh yes, that's who He is." They'd been fraught with worry, and giving in to the worries, this was what they got. Anxiety and worry are not trustworthy guides.

If Jesus's own parents couldn't understand who Jesus was at that moment, can we always be sure our own loved ones know us at the core of our being? All our upbringing might have been perfect and loving, but we can't let that define us, because we aren't simply someone's daughter or son or sister or brother. We must lose ourselves to find ourselves. Jesus was the son of a carpenter, but then did he dutifully take over the family business, running it and growing it? No. At around age thirty he set out on his calling, leaving home.

Even then, he had to lose himself before launching his ministry, spending forty days in the wilderness, without any food or any friends joining him. I've already discussed the poignancy and pain of that loneliness, facing up to the devil's temptations. It was all part of the work of losing himself as he found himself.

Most often when we're so-called "finding our life" we're doing it for ourselves and our own selfish reasons. And yet, when we do just the opposite, we can do it for Jesus and for God. Enhancing our self-image can be a source of motivation, but think about it—how long does that usually last? The pleasure of patting yourself on the back tends to be short-lived, lest you become that one who broke his arm patting himself on the back. (We used to practice that gesture in high school, quite literally, just to say sarcastically, "See, aren't I great?") My warning to self: If you're too sure of yourself, Rick, think again. Look harder. Look beyond yourself. Lose something of yourself. Who knows what you might gain?

To know is to not know. That can be profound.

REFLECTIONS FOR MODERN LIVING

- Is it possible that we spend so much time trying to find ourselves that we forget to see the power of losing ourselves?
- Have you ever witnessed someone bottoming out?
- What would you look to letting go of, if you could?
- Are there things you desperately cling to that get in the way of you trusting God completely?

33

KEEP AT IT

Jesus tells a good story, reminding us of how we need to keep at it and never lose heart. There was a judge, an unjust judge, who was badgered by a widow who kept coming back to him, begging for justice. We're left to wonder what exactly her opponent has done. What's important is her persistence. And it pays off. The unjust judge simply gives up, or gives in. He knows she'll keep coming back and simply wear him out. Enough already.

Note: He is unjust, not a good guy. He gives in for the most selfish and self-protective of reasons. Well, then, think about the Lord, remember how good and fair he is. When a widow with such persistence comes to God, God answers. There's also an important societal contrast in the story that we might lose. A widow in Jesus's time was among the most vulnerable. She doesn't have a pension or trust fund to pay for a lawyer or a bundle of stocks to cash in. All she has is herself and her belief in what needs to be done. She doesn't give up. We shouldn't either. People who persist in the right things are heard.

Persistence in prayer can lead to a better understanding of what you really need, not a superficial want, but a big need. As you pray over time—don't give up—you gain a deeper understanding of what you're really missing. Maybe initially the prayer is: "God, please make sure my boss gives me a really good raise." No doubt about it, the need is there. But as you persist, sometimes a deeper need will reveal itself. You need more money, yes, but you also need to know you're doing what you're called to do, where your gifts can serve you and others best, where you can be who you're meant to be. How very satisfying. A prayer that might seem selfish at the start—don't stop yourself—can lead you to dig even deeper.

You're being given a chance to be transformed, and the change might be bigger than you could have ever expected. Jesus gives us new and vivid analogies. No one sews an "unshrunk cloth" on an old cloak, he says. I mean, wouldn't I put a new elbow patch on my old tweed jacket (how cool that would be)? The key word here is "unshrunk." It's not going to fit. It's going to come off in time.

Or to take a better analogy, especially for any vintners among us (speak up), no one puts new wine into old wineskins, as Jesus said. Why? Because the fresh wine would break the skins, the wine would spill out, and it would all be lost. You put new wine into new, fresh wineskins. Don't cling to the old. Be ready for the new that can renew you at any age. When you hear yourself thinking or saying, "But we've always done it this way," maybe there's a better new way. Look for it. Open yourself to it.

We think we can twist things around for our own benefit, but Jesus knows better. He can anticipate the narrowness of our thinking. He'll tell a story, a parable, and as we listen to it and empathize—the gift of story—we can discover a whole new way of thinking. Did Jesus really say that God was like an unjust judge? Not exactly. But the story told us how *we* can change, how we can grow, our persistence in prayer paying off.

When we watch a movie or a TV show, we think we know who the bad guy is. The cleverest of shows can surprise us, keep us hanging on till that last episode.

There's a rich man who has a manager handling his property—a money manager of sorts, with much more tangible items than stocks and bonds. He's heard that the guy was squandering things. (Get him on the phone.) He calls the man forward and asks, "What is this that I hear? Give me an accounting of what you're doing. You can't be my manager any longer." Okay, it's a setup. That guy must be the bad guy.

The manager doesn't want to lose his job. He doesn't want to have to do manual labor or, worse, become a beggar. He's crafty and comes up with a plan. Anything he can do to add to his reputation or at least help him get another job. (Certainly, we've never had such untoward thoughts for ourselves—or have we? Desperation can know no bounds.)

He goes to his master's debtors and asks them how much they owe the man. One says, "A hundred jugs of olive oil." The unjust manager says, "Take your bill, sit down quickly and make it fifty." He asks another. "A hundred containers of wheat," the man replies. "Take your bill and make it eighty."

Was he doing something good for his boss? Not at all, not in the least. But he was—selfishly, brazenly—looking out for himself. If or when he was fired and had to go looking for a new job, he'd have a pretty passel of supporters who could put in a good word for him. "Remember that favor I did for *you*?" he'd remind them. "Can you do a big favor for *me*?" One good—or bad—deed deserves another.

Now here's the twist. We would expect the boss to be livid when he discovers what the soon-to-be-fired manager had done. On the contrary, the boss is impressed by the manager's shrewdness. It makes you wonder what kind of "shrewd" tactics the boss had used to acquire *his* riches. Takes one to know one. Or perhaps it's just an act of generosity on his part.

What a puzzling story. Neither of the main characters seem like models of behavior. What they are is crafty, crafty about worldly goods. And that's exactly the point Jesus is making. We might give the story a smile. We've known cagey characters like that—not that we're like that ourselves. But Jesus pulled us in to think more deeply about ourselves. As he wryly notes, "I tell you, make friends for yourselves by means of dishonest wealth so that when it is gone, they may welcome you in the eternal homes."

When it is gone. Wealth, honest or dishonest, doesn't last forever. We don't get to take it with us after we're gone. In another story Jesus tells of a rich man who pulls down his old barns to build bigger ones to store an abundance of grain and crops, more than he'd ever had before. Now he can eat, drink, and be merry forever (all those massive investments). Uh-oh, guess what? Just then God calls him home, dying on the vine. Better to build up riches in heaven than here on earth. Be that persistent widow praying. Turn yourself into a new wineskin, ready for new wine.

We spend so much time and energy being crafty about material things, about our wealth, how to make it grow, gauging what investments to make, where we should spend it and cash in. Why can't we be just as focused, just as clever, just as demanding about spiritual things, choosing to make ourselves grow? Wealth is a dishonest master. God never is.

REFLECTIONS FOR MODERN LIVING

- Do you ever find yourself repeating the same prayer?
- Do you tend to separate your "business self" from your spiritual self?
- Where do you struggle with persistence?
- Is that old wineskin—that old self-image—keeping you from welcoming the good new wine that the Lord is offering?

34

LET'S DO IT TOGETHER

It's an often-quoted line from Jesus: "For where two or three are gathered in my name, I am there among them." Two or three or more, that's something. So often today in the context of modern, present-day spirituality, the emphasis is on the lone seeker. Going off by yourself to seek the truth. Facing your demons one-on-one. Giving yourself private meditation time and prayer. I don't want to discount that. After all, we've seen how Jesus needed to go off by himself to connect and reconnect with God, getting away from the crowd.

But here's another insight to spiritual growth, so crucial to us. Faith is something that we do in community. Growing close to Jesus, seeking him out, understanding him, comes when two or three or more are gathered. Jesus is there with us. When it says "in my name" the setup is also clear. We must be honest about Whose will we seek, Whose friends we are and wish to be, Whom we yearn to follow.

Jesus didn't leave behind a big book for all of us to read. We know what he said and what he did all these years later because of what his followers passed along and wrote down. Jesus didn't leave behind a building or series of buildings. He didn't create some elegant administrative plan for x and y to do z. He didn't establish a constitution explaining how things

would run when he was gone from this earth, looking down on us from heaven.

What he had were followers, men and women—we must never forget the women; including them, as he did, was hugely countercultural. It was a patriarchal society back in the day. With Jesus, the one patriarch that truly mattered was and is the Father, his father, our father. Following Jesus is something we're meant to do together. The church, for all its failings, is exactly that, Jesus's followers coming together, seeking his will, studying his words, praying for each other. When two or more are gathered in Jesus's name, they can't but help pray for the world, for themselves, for each other. For when two or more are gathered, sharing their needs and concerns, they will inevitably pray for each other.

Taking it in context, this line from the book of Matthew comes after advice Jesus gives about what to do when conflicts between his followers arise. It's very practical advice. First go for a one-on-one conversation, where you point out how you have been hurt. It's very possible that the other has been unaware of their doings, their sins (to use a word). If the person listens and understands, that's good enough. If not, "take one or two others along with you, so that every word may be confirmed by the evidence of two or three witnesses."

If that doesn't work, tell it to the whole group—the church, say. If the offending party refuses to listen even to the church, then as Jesus says, "Let such a one be to you as a Gentile and a tax collector." (Even as I type those words, I am indeed reminded of how Jesus offended so many by communing with those very tax collectors.) Jesus is offering up strategies for group management and cohesiveness. What it requires is commitment and, dare I stress it again, incredible honesty. Alas, in church, too often politeness—with some rolling of eyes in the pews and whispering on the side—reigns over accountability.

Jesus knew that getting along together in a group is not always easy.

Twelve-step groups are designed around these very principles. Like I said, I haven't been a member of such a group, but I've known many whose lives have been transformed by them. Honesty and accountability are right at the top of the list, along with relinquishing to "a Power greater than ourselves" for change. We all have failings. We need each other to be reminded of them, to be called on the carpet, to be able to come clean.

"Truly I tell you," Jesus goes on to say, "whatever you bind on earth will be bound in heaven, and whatever you loose on earth will be loosed in heaven." All this hard work we have to do with each other is mirrored in the beyond. It's not just tough-love meetings behind closed doors, with gritted teeth, painful words, and maybe some tears—may they be healing tears. God is present right there. Where two or three are gathered, after all.

In another passage, this from the Gospel of Mark, we read how Jesus sent out his disciples "two by two." Wait, Jesus, is that such a good idea? we might wonder. If he only had twelve disciples and they go two-by-two, isn't he limiting the ground they might be able to cover? They could go twice as far if they went out one-by-one. But Jesus knows his followers. He knows *us*. Our power increases in community. Just look at what he was sending along with them, "authority over unclean spirits."

They would be able to "cast out demons," a phrase that makes me think of Jesus and his followers as the first psychotherapists, years before Freud. They were armed to help those with mental maladies as well as cure the sick, and they will do it two-by-two. The work of a therapist can be extremely stressful. Some of the therapists I know are in shared practices so they can talk to a compatriot about their work, to compare notes, to ask for guidance, to be reassured they are doing it right. Or they have colleagues they can consult. In my work life, as a writer and editor, I would have been lost—or at least failed miserably—without wise and helpful colleagues. I had the privilege of working with some talented people. It's sort of like playing tennis, where playing with someone good can raise your game.

You want to follow Jesus? Do it in community. Join a Bible study. Join a church. Join a fellow follower or two for regular get-togethers and prayer. Jesus will be there with you.

REFLECTIONS FOR MODERN LIVING

- Is there someone you can trust when you need to talk about anything?
- Do you ever see how "two or more are gathered" by Zoom or email?
- Can social media be a place where "two or more are gathered," or is it a distraction from the same?
- How have interactions with other people enhanced your spiritual life?

35

JESUS IS THE WAY

Those earliest Christians were often called "People of the Way," and would refer to themselves that way. In the book of Acts, which recounts the events that led to the spread of Christianity in the ancient Roman world, the term is used a couple of times. For instance, the apostle Paul, then named Saul, was searching out "any who belonged to the Way," so they could be called forward, harassed, and punished, all before he had his remarkable conversion experience.

The word itself, of course, comes right out of the mouth of Jesus with his stunning declaration in the Gospel of John: "I am the way, and the truth, and the life. No one comes to the Father except through me." It's easy enough to get mired in the seeming exclusivity of that route, *No one comes to the Father.* I've heard it used to justify a "I'm right; you're wrong" attitude of faith. After all, didn't Jesus say that "no one" could come to the Father except through him? Therefore, we've got it all right and everybody else is going to hell. So there.

The thing that makes me wary about that kind of thinking is that Jesus himself was given to challenge all those who seemed so unarguably certain of themselves. Is that really the best way to love our neighbor? Can we always listen closely like

that? Is that the best way to seep ourselves in compassion or even pray?

When you get to know Jesus and keep trying to know him better, you see that he isn't just a preacher/teacher laying out some quick gridwork for salvation. He is so much bigger than that, a luminous being practicing miracles left and right, challenging the prejudices and wrongful thinking of his era. He had such a brief time on earth, only three years of active ministry, whereas everything he said and did is worthy of a lifetime of contemplation. Jesus isn't some cartoon figure gesturing to a sign that points the way; he *is* the way . . . and the truth and the life. Wow, that's not simply a "my way or the highway" statement. It's about living with a being who *is* God on earth. He and God are one and the same. "Whoever welcomes you welcomes me," he said to the disciples as he sent them out. "And whoever welcomes me welcomes the one who sent me."

This can be unspeakably hard for us to grasp. We want to put people—and God—in boxes. "Okay, God, you're up there and we're down here." Jesus just flipped it around. God is right here on earth for us to follow. He knew what it was like to live with the temptations of everyday life, the greed and anger that was all around. He was unashamed to show anger himself, tapping into that most human of emotions. That image of the sweet, saintly man welcoming children with open arms gets modified when we read of his going into the temple only days before he was crucified and overturning the tables of the money changers, people who were taking advantage of others and profiting by it.

I like to picture his angry face as he said, "It is written, 'My house shall be called a house of prayer,'" quoting Scripture. He then says, "But you are making it a den of robbers." He is rightly furious. And to clarify his values he then cured the lame and the blind, who were usually excluded from the temple. Is it any wonder that those in power felt threatened?

Is this the Way? Yes. Is this the truth and the life showing itself? Indeed yes.

A few days later, when Jesus knew, as only he could know, the horrors of what he was about to face, the humiliation of being abandoned by those he loved and who followed him—look how many times Peter denied knowing him—and the misery of hanging from a cross for hours until he would die, he prayed, as any of us would pray, "My Father, if it is possible, let this cup pass from me." No, God, no. Wouldn't any of us ask the same, don't let me die in excruciating pain like this? Then in the same sentence, separated by one of the biggest semicolons in history, he went on to say, "Yet not what I want but what you want."

He is the way showing us the way. *Not what we want but what God wants.* That's got to be the hardest prayer on earth, such a moment of relinquishment. Much of its power derives from the first part of the sentence. Faith can come when we reveal all that we are and expose our true selves—not what we want people to think, but what we are.

In one account we learn that Jesus, when praying in the garden hours before his death, addressed God the Father in the most intimate of terms, calling him "Abba" which would be almost like saying "Daddy." And later, the apostle Paul, writing to the People of the Way in Rome, says, "When we cry 'Abba! Father!' it is that very Spirit bearing witness with our spirit that we are children of God." We are empowered to use that same intimate language.

The Lord's Prayer, the prayer Jesus gave us, opens with a similar sort of address. "Our Father," we say, calling on God. He's not just Jesus's father; he is Our Father. And if you wanted to call him Daddy, I don't think he would be shocked.

Think again of that story, surely apocryphal, of someone asking a great composer—Beethoven or Brahms, someone of that exalted stature—what a certain phrase in a piece meant. The great composer sat down and played the whole piece over again.

Jesus is the Way? Yes, Jesus is the way and the truth and the life. And if you want to find out exactly what that way is, there isn't any blinders-on shortcut. Because each little thing we learn, each anecdote, each parable, each phrase, each moment, fills in the whole picture. We are people of the Way when we look to all that and seek to put it into practice in our own lives. We can follow Jesus by following and following and following. It's not just about observing a list of rules and practices. Jesus IS the way. Let's go for it.

REFLECTIONS FOR MODERN LIVING

- Have you ever prayed the Jesus prayer "Jesus Christ, have mercy upon me?"
- Do you avoid or repress your anger rather than express it openly, as Jesus did?
- Who in your life shows you the way to the Way?
- We see Jesus expressing himself intimately in prayer, calling God "Abba"—can you?

36

WHEN *IS* NOW

There is a natural human urge to have our life's schedule all spelled out and the calendar well marked. How long do we have to work before retirement? When will the Social Security benefits kick in? When is the best time to have a kid or when should that kid start school? Maybe we should hold him back for a year. How many years do I have left? Can I stick this job out till I get a promotion? Would that we got an Excel spreadsheet right at the start. It would make things so much easier.

Or would it really? Is that the best way to live? Gazing too long at the crystal ball might distract us from savoring each moment we're given. Instead of asking "What's next?" maybe it's better to think, "What can I do *now*?"

Jesus lived in tumultuous times, just as we often feel we are living in the most tumultuous times. Whether the threat is a nuclear holocaust, predictions of global warming, or a worldwide pandemic, we read of people stocking up on months of canned goods or digging a shelter where they can hide out until the disaster—whatever it is—has passed. The Romans had taken over Jerusalem in 63 B.C.E., and the wily and violent Herod ruled the land shortly before Jesus's birth. The Romans sent their own governors, like Pontius Pilate, and used some of

the locals to collect taxes, i.e., the reviled tax collectors, hated because they were infamous for skimming off the top, or bottom, for themselves.

Resistance to Roman rule was pervasive, and things exploded into open rebellion in 66 A.D., after Jesus's death, a war that came to a dramatic end when Rome destroyed the temple in Jerusalem in 70 A.D. Paul's letters in the New Testament were written before then. Of the four Gospels, Mark is the earliest, probably written around 70 A.D. or a little before then. The other three were written after. So, does that mean we can take their predictions of a coming disaster with a grain of salt—after all, they were recorded when fate had taken its toll? Or can we trust that they are recording things that were said and passed on orally for years? Remember, it was long before the printed word, in an era when some of the greatest poetry was passed down through remembered words.

When you couldn't look things up in a book—or a Google search—you would have to be savvier about verbal memory. In a distant era when most had to learn things through memorization, they were no doubt better at it than we are. They couldn't open a file drawer or pull down a book from the shelf, let alone log on to a computer.

Jesus seems to have accurately foretold some of the disasters that would take place. He pointed at the buildings of the temple, which his followers could gaze at in awe—it was God's home, a sacred place. "You see all these, do you not?" he asked them. "Truly I tell you, not one stone will be left here upon another, all will be thrown down." Words that would prove all too true. As for his own fate, he could foresee and openly explain, getting down to the exact dates on the Jewish calendar, "You know that after two days the Passover is coming, and the Son of Man will be handed over to be crucified." It would happen all too soon.

Jesus doesn't make it any easier for his disciples—or us. They follow him to the Mount of Olives to get more details. Surely, they could be given some heavenly sign, some indication that the moment was coming, the way we'd look to an app on our phones for what the weather will be, that storm that has a 50 percent chance of coming (if you're like me, choosing the app's expertise rather than gazing out the window at the sky).

Yes, Jesus says, they would hear of wars and rumors of wars—we know what that's like—but they wouldn't take place, not just yet. (How accurate are the news cycles at predicting, anyway?) "For nation will rise against nation," he says, "and kingdom against kingdom, and there will be famines and earthquakes in various places; all this is but the beginning of the birth pangs." What, Lord? You mean there will be some good to come out of this? Really?

Evidently not for them, not in the long haul. "Then they will hand you over to be tortured and will put you to death," Jesus goes on to say, "and you will be hated by all nations because of my name." By most accounts, some of it biblical, some of it tradition, eleven of the twelve disciples ended up being martyred. They also spread the good news, as Jesus promised, showing their dedication and resilience. "And this good news of the kingdom will be proclaimed throughout the world, as a testimony to all the nations"—good so far—"and then the end will come." Ugh, there it is, that apocryphal end that gets even more juice in the last book in the Bible, Revelation.

In the Gospels, what we call the Good News, you can hear the disciples yearning to know when, just when. Signs, signs, they wonder, couldn't they be given signs? "When you see the desolating sacrilege, standing in the holy place," Jesus says, "then those in Judea must flee to the mountains." A desolating sacrilege would probably have meant an altar or statue to a pagan god in the temple, something drastically unholy. When that happened, there wasn't a moment to lose. "The one on the housetop must not go down to take what is in the house; the one in the field must not turn back to get a coat. Woe to those who are pregnant and to those who are nursing infants." This all sounds awful coming from the prince of peace. But then for the elect, he says, at least "those days will be cut short."

All this talk from Jesus doesn't seem like it's about looking at the future as much as it is about noticing the present. They were to take note of false prophets, trying to lead them astray. "For as the lightning comes from the east and flashes as far as the west, so will be the coming of the Son of Man," Jesus says in what is probably a reference to his own coming. Did they pay attention, are they still paying attention, are we? "Wherever the corpse is, there the vultures will gather." You can chew on bad news like a vulture, but can you see the good that is coming?

"Immediately after the suffering of those days, the sun will be darkened, and the moon will not give its light; the stars will fall from heaven, and the power of heaven will be shaken," Jesus says. "Then the sign of the Son of Man will appear in heaven." Note: The Son of Man's coming *is* a sign. That's something they've already seen and experienced with Jesus here on earth. They've seen that sign. "And then all the tribes of the earth will mourn, and they will see 'the Son of Man coming on the clouds of heaven' with power and great glory. And he will send out his angels with a loud trumpet call, and they will gather his elect from the four winds, from one end of heaven to the other."

It's glorious and confusing at the same time. There is a coming, then some monstrous end times, and then a coming again. When? When will it be? Even in the relatively brief period of American history, there have been predictions and more predictions about exact dates and times, all of them proving disastrously wrong about when Jesus would return. If we can't know, or these good, carefully exacting believers can't know, how can anyone know? It's that Excel spreadsheet in the brain that's yearning to be satisfied. Jesus is not here for that. His message goes way deeper.

In the end Jesus won't say exactly when. "Truly I tell you, this generation will not pass away until all these things have taken place. Heaven and earth will pass away, but my words will not pass away." Prediction enough with a satisfying albeit scary promise, and yet as he says, "But about that day and hour no one knows, neither the angels of heaven, nor the Son, but only the Father." If Jesus himself can't know, how can we?

All we can do is see what is before us. Beware of things that lead us astray, liars and cheats that twist things around, appealing to the worst sides of our nature. Look away from the app that thinks it knows everything. Turn the page from the frightening, exhausting news story. Watch out for the know-it-all on social media. Signs can be distracting and wrong. No need for a sign. Jesus is here right now. That's what we need to pay attention to.

Reflections for Modern Living

- Do you ever wish you had an accurate, trustworthy Excel spreadsheet in your brain?
- Whose financial predictions of the future are you inclined to trust?
- Do you change your behavior when you read about things like global warming?
- Has your life followed an expected course?

37

We Might Lose Him. He Won't Lose Us.

As much as Jesus tried to prepare his followers for what would happen to him, they struggled to believe it. We shouldn't feel bad as we struggle to believe. He said it straight out, referring to himself in the third person (would that have made it easier to take in?). "The Son of Man is going to be betrayed into human hands, and they will kill him, and on the third day he will be raised." How distressing. Wouldn't you be disturbed if your beloved teacher said such a thing, after all the risks you had taken to follow him?

The death part, the monstrous killing, must have been the most upsetting. But what about that promise that he would be raised on the last day? What on earth could that mean? Maybe he's saying, "Stick around, I'll show you." Hadn't they seen amazing things already? The miracles of healing, his casting out of demons, the feeding of the five thousand and the four thousand, his raising the dead back to life. And that extraordinary moment, only witnessed by three of them—the Transfiguration—when his clothes turned a dazzling white and two prophets, Moses and Elijah, appeared with him, and a voice from heaven proclaimed, "This is my Son, listen to him!" They did listen, but there was so much to take in.

Is it any wonder that when that third day finally came and he rose from the dead, they could barely understand? He had died, a terrible death, as predicted. That was surely what stayed in their heads, coupled perhaps with some guilt that they hadn't done anything to stop it (risking the chance of getting killed or maimed in the process). They lost him. They were lost.

It was the women who went to the tomb first. The specifics vary from Gospel to Gospel, but note it was always women there first, women who braved the trip, bringing spices that they might put on the dead body, wondering how on earth they would push aside the heavy stone from the entrance of the tomb. What a shock to discover the stone was already rolled aside, and there was no body inside. Was this one more disaster to face up to?

They were greeted—by exactly who depends on which Gospel you are reading. Matthews says it was an angel, Mark says it was a young man, Luke says there were two men, and John depicts two angels. What matters most is what they were told. Jesus of Nazareth was not there. He had risen from the dead, as he had promised. They were to pass on the news to the disciples.

Mark is sometimes called the unfinished Gospel because in its earliest version, the women fled from the tomb in terror and amazement and didn't tell anyone out of abject fear. That was that. In the Gospel of Luke, we read that the apostles refused to believe the news, mere idle talk—from women, mind you. Peter rushed back to see for himself, looking into the empty tomb where all that lay were the linen cloths. He was amazed.

In John's version, which sticks in my head because of how it was sung by the choir one Easter Sunday morning, Mary Magdalene sees the empty tomb, alerts Peter and "the other disciple, the one whom Jesus loved." That has traditionally been considered a reference to John, although it's a little weird to think of Jesus showing such favoritism. Maybe that favoritism was justified because although Peter sees the linen wrapping lying on the floor, and in a lovely detail, the cloth that had been on Jesus's head all rolled up, it's the disciple "whom Jesus loved" who gets to the tomb first. He looks in, sees, and believes.

Not given to lingering, the men go off, leaving Mary there by herself, weeping. The two angels ask her why she is crying. "They have taken away my Lord, and I do not know where they have laid him," she says. She turns around and sees Jesus standing there and doesn't recognize him—not the first time such a thing will happen. How could she have not known him, even when he speaks, asking her why she's weeping? Didn't she recognize that compassionate voice and/or that face? Instead, she mistakes him for the gardener and asks him to tell her where they have taken her Lord, her anxiety and sorrow blinding her.

Only when he says her name, "Mary," does she know it is he. He has called her by name, as he calls all of us. "Rabbouni!" she replies in Hebrew, a significant response in this culture where at the time of Jesus, Aramaic was the spoken language, Hebrew the word of the Scriptures. "Teacher!" she has exclaimed, as though acknowledging in one powerful word his fulfilling of the Scriptural promise.

You know she wants to grasp him, hold him tight, but he warns her, no, not now, he is here on earth, but only temporarily. She might have still wondered, why didn't she recognize him? She knew him so well and loved him. Maybe it's because to truly believe and accept the mystery of the Resurrection is hard, even for his first-century followers.

That same day, Sunday, the first day of the week, he appears to some of his disciples who are hiding in a house behind locked doors. "Peace be with you," he says and shows them his hands and his side. He reminds them of their calling; as the Father has sent him, he sends them. And then breathes on them the power of the Holy Spirit, reminding them that if they forgive the sins of any, those sins will be forgiven.

Thomas, now universally known as Doubting Thomas, was not there for this event. He doesn't believe the account his fellow disciples have given and stubbornly declares, "Unless I see the mark of the nails in his hands and put my finger in the mark of the nails and my hand in his side"—where Jesus was wounded—"I will not believe." Don't we know the feeling? "Show me," we want to say. Show me, Lord.

I don't think we should trash the value of doubting. In fact, it can go hand-in-hand with faith. Not for nothing was Thomas called the Twin, a man with two sides, the faithful side ultimately winning out. Don't hide your doubts, confront them. As the brilliant author Frederick Buechner once said, "Doubts are the ants in the pants of faith. They keep it awake and moving." Doubts and faith, curious adversaries and bedfellows.

All these devoted followers of Jesus, they think they have lost him, but he hasn't lost them. Sure enough, when he appears to Thomas, he invites the doubting soul to put his fingers where the wounds were and feel Jesus's side. "Do not doubt but believe," Jesus says. At once that's enough for Thomas. He doesn't need more evidence than that. "My Lord and my God," he says. Would that it could be good enough for the rest of us. "Blessed are those who have not seen," Jesus says, "and yet have come to believe." That's us.

To take another instance where Jesus was not recognized, let's go to the Gospel of Luke. Two of his followers were walking on the road to Emmaus, about seven miles from Jerusalem, and talking about what had just happened, the brutal Crucifixion. They are joined by a third, Jesus himself. No introductions are made. Their eyes are blinded anyway, no doubt by pain and sorrow. Indeed, our emotions can blind us. When Jesus asks them what they're discussing, they "stood still, looking sad." It is Cleopas, one of the two, who asks, "Are you the only stranger in Jerusalem who does not know the things that have taken place there in these days?" "What things?" Jesus asks.

I don't think he's simply being sly. Telling and retelling the events of those days was crucial to the news being passed along and eventually recorded in the Gospels. That the versions might differ in detail doesn't bother me. The big picture is there: Jesus was raised from the dead. Easter is here. Those women who went to the tomb early that morning spoke of the stone being rolled away, Jesus's body missing, and the vision they had of angels saying that he was still alive. Others went to the tomb, too, to verify what the women had said—you needed to see something like that with your own eyes.

There on the road to Emmaus Jesus responds, challenging them, as though he's thinking, *Come on, you guys, remember this stuff, remember all that I taught you; you'll need to pass it on.* "Oh, how foolish you are, and how slow of heart to believe all that the prophets have declared!" he says. "Was it not necessary that the Messiah should suffer these things and then enter into his glory?" The good Teacher goes back and reviews all that was prophesized in Scripture.

Clearly their hearts were warmed, as we're later told, because instead of sending Jesus on his way or just ignoring all this talk, they invite him to come with them. It's getting late and he'll need a place to stay. They hadn't forgotten what he had taught them, to welcome the stranger, to offer food and comfort. It was only then, sitting at the table with them, when he took bread, blessed it, and broke it—as he had done only days before at the Last Supper—that their eyes were opened. It was he; it was Jesus. And with that, he vanished from their sight.

At last, they knew it was true. They rushed back to Jerusalem and shared the news. Jesus was risen. They'd seen it with their own eyes—when their eyes were finally opened. He broke bread with them and then was gone. As though to reiterate the news, Jesus himself appears. "Peace be with you," he says. Peace, because the whole thing could still be frightening.

I find these incidents of recognizing and not recognizing reassuring. Jesus knows how human we are, how we yearn for material evidence. He also knows how we can lose sight of things, the deeper mystical truths of life. Take heart. He simply never loses sight of us.

REFLECTIONS FOR MODERN LIVING

- Do you struggle with doubt even as you believe?
- When you hear of some miracle, do you trust the narrative or wish for tangible evidence?
- Do you always recognize Jesus's presence?
- What reassuring signs have you had of Jesus at work in your life or the lives of others?

38

YOUR UNEXPECTED NEIGHBOR

Okay, we know we're supposed to love our neighbor as ourselves. We've got that, Jesus; we'll try to do our best. But then, we might ask, as did a lawyer in the Gospel of Luke, "Who is my neighbor?"

I live in a wonderful neighborhood. My wife and I have lived here almost forty years. We raised our kids here. They played in the local kids' baseball league (that I happened to co-found, mostly because I'm so lousy at baseball I needed to recruit other dads and moms to help!). They got on the school bus at the corner. They played in the playground. They walked to their friends' houses for playdates and walked home. We can't step out of the door without seeing many a familiar face, stopping to chat a bit on the way to the store or the local pharmacy. These are my neighbors, easy enough to love. I trust they'd do anything for me as I would do anything for them. During tough times, an illness, say, or a kid's broken limb, they have reached out, dropping off dinner at our front door or bringing a fragrant bouquet of flowers, sending notes, showing up at a hospital bedside. How blessed we are.

Living here this long, we've also seen how the neighborhood has changed over the years. In the aftermath of World War II and even before, it became a refuge for German Jews, their new home far from home. Frankfurt on the Hudson it was dubbed. You'd see copies of the *Frankfurter Allgemeine Zeitung*, the German newspaper, and a few Yiddish papers. Our lovely next-door neighbor Hildegarde, albeit not Jewish, had survived the bombing of Frankfurt by the Allies when she was a girl. A knock on our door from her only meant good things. We still have a few pieces of furniture that she gave us when she and her husband moved into an elder home, including two beautiful chests of drawers.

As those dear souls have died, the foreign languages I'm more likely to hear on the neighborhood streets are Russian and Spanish. I listen to the former, trying desperately to understand, if I could only grasp a word or two. I listen to the latter, largely settlers from the Dominican Republic, with a little more comprehension from my knowledge of Italian and French. In fact, I'll sometimes take a stab at speaking in Italian to one of my Spanish-speaking neighbors, the two languages are close enough. I also like volunteering at the English as a Second Language (ESL) classes that we teach at our church, one-on-one sessions in the sanctuary with neighbors who come from as far away as China and want to learn and/or improve their English. When they look at me quizzically, uncomprehendingly, I think, "Would that we all had the gift of tongues."

Having grown up in a largely homogenous suburb of Los Angeles (one that has changed immensely since I moved away), I confess I've had moments when I wish that some of my neighbors followed some of those unspoken rules I grew up with. "Would you please turn down your car radio?" I'll think when that guy drives by, his music playing full blast with the windows down. Meanwhile, I have reveled in the music that comes from the pen of another neighbor, Lin Manuel Miranda, whose Broadway musical *Hamilton* rocked my soul and whose first big work, *In the Heights*, was about the very neighborhood we live in—okay maybe not our exact block but just a street or two away. See, I'm already redefining the hood.

All of it makes me want to pause and rethink that question, "Who is my neighbor?" My knee-jerk reaction is that my neighbor is somebody who is a lot like me, who understands what I'm talking about without my overexplaining, who probably votes just like I do when we step into the voting booth (at our neighborhood school), who'd be comfortable in our church. And then I recall stories I've heard from some in our beloved faith community, people of color, who have gone to look at an apartment that was available to near the church. All was fine on the initial phone call, but when they showed up, they were told, "It's no longer available."

Heartbreaking.

Jesus tells a story—that's just what Jesus does—of a man on a road trip who is attacked by robbers. They beat him up and just leave him there, at the side of the street, half dead. Okay, now, who are his neighbors? This will be the test. Will it be the priest, a holy man, who when he sees this victim, crosses by on the other side of the road? Or perhaps it would be a Levite, a teacher of the law, who does just the same, crosses over to the other side, to avoid the victim. It is the third passerby—these things often come in threes—a hated and vilified Samaritan, one who has followed the wrong way, who stops. Filled with pity, he bandages the victim's wounds, pouring oil and wine on them, then puts him on the back of his animal, a donkey, say, and takes him to an inn and looks over him, delaying his own trip by a day. He gives some money to the innkeeper and promises that he'll come back and repay the innkeeper whatever additional expenses there are.

He is the good Samaritan—or Good Samaritan—nomenclature that has been amplified and raised to glory through its use as the name for many a hospital or clinic where people are healed and cared for. We don't even hear anymore the tension in those two words that would have been there for Jesus's listeners. Samaritans were not considered good. Jesus doesn't call him "good" in the story. It's not what he is; it's what he does.

That's who our neighbor is, the one we are to love as we love ourselves. Not unlike Jesus's listeners, we can easily separate people into "them" versus "us." We often do it unconsciously, quick judgments and classifications to streamline our lives. We give someone a label so we won't have to dig deeper to figure out who they might really be. We can even give ourselves labels, claiming membership and identity here or there. Watch out. The one who can save your life might not at all be whom you expect, sheer generosity coming from "the wrong place."

I try to keep some one-dollar bills in my pocket to give to whomever might ask for a buck (or two) outside the subway station, on the train, or near the church. And note, lest you think I'm an outrageously generous fellow, it's usually just a one. "You don't want to do that," someone will tell me. "They'll just take your money and spend it on drugs. Tell them to just come to the soup kitchen." I do that too. But that dollar in someone's cup or hand is not so much for them as for me. I don't want to walk on by, labeling them "beggar." I want to see a person. What do I know led to their situation? I rarely find out. But I pray for some interaction. "God bless you," is most often the response. How often do you hear a stranger say that to you? I can be—they can be—a neighbor.

REFLECTIONS FOR MODERN LIVING

- Have you learned new things by interacting with people from different backgrounds or cultures?
- As you consider Jesus's command to love your neighbor as yourself, do you ever ask, "Who is my neighbor?"
- Why can it be so hard to love a neighbor who is not like you?
- How can you make sure you recognize the goodness of those Good Samaritans in your life?

39

PEACE WILL COME

Don't I yearn for it? Don't you? Can't we all get along? I'm not even thinking of the devastating wars that pop up all over the world—every time we believe we've entered a period of worldly peace, there seems to be another war, large and small—I'm thinking of the conflicts and demonization that can happen neighbor to neighbor, family to family, friend to friend.

Prince of Peace is one of those titles Jesus bears, one that isn't found in the Gospels at all but in the book of Isaiah: "For a child has been born for us, a son given to us; authority rests upon his shoulders; and he is named Wonderful Counselor, Mighty God, Everlasting Father, Prince of Peace." As I write the words down, I can hear them sung, set to music in Handel's *Messiah* (with Handel putting a pause between "Wonderful" and "Counselor" as if they were two nouns and not an adjective describing a noun).

Jesus's early followers were awaiting that Messiah, one who would put an end to the power structures of the day. The Roman rulers would finally be banished; in place of a Caesar, they'd have their own leader sitting on a throne. "Blessed are the peacemakers," Jesus says, "for they will be called children of God." That sounds pretty good. Sign me up. And then I think

about just how much work that takes. I mean, just settling some conflict at work, gathering the troops together, working out the differences. Ugh. Or worse, calming the storms that might be brewing at home. Not to mention the "us versus them" language that assaults us every time we log onto the news. Peacemaker . . . can't someone else do it?

Look how Jesus put it: "Peace I leave with you; my peace I give to you. I do not give to you as the world gives. Do not let your hearts be troubled, and do not let them be afraid." Pause on that. Go out for a walk and reflect on it. Let the message fill you up, cleaning out the annoyances that have been keeping house. Say a prayer. Let Jesus do the work, the heavy lifting. *Do not let your hearts be troubled.* That can mean giving up a lot of our preconceptions.

Think about what Jesus's first followers had to do. First off, they struggled to truly comprehend that he was the Messiah. Jesus asked the disciples what other people called him, who they thought he was. The answers were many: some said John the Baptist, others Elijah or Jeremiah (as though there was some sort of reincarnation). Then Jesus got more specific: "But who do *you* say that I am?" (Italics added for emphasis.)

"You are the Messiah," Peter said.

Right answer, Peter, but in one of those unexpected responses, Jesus told them not to tell anyone about him. They had to keep it a secret, at least for now, that he was the Messiah—how baffling. When Jesus went on to recount the horrors that awaited him, that he would be tried and killed, Peter immediately objected, full of compassion. "God forbid it, Lord!" he said. "This must never happen to you." Wrong response, Peter. "Get behind me, Satan!" Jesus said. Peter, who had gotten it right the first time around, was now on the wrong track. "You are setting your mind not on divine things," Jesus continued, "but on human things."

You can feel them struggling to get their heads around it. That heroic Messiah, the general of the troops who would triumph over the enemy forces, that worldly king, that earthly power, this wasn't who Jesus was. Peace was not going to come that way. It never does. Violence begats more violence, displays of power invite more of the same.

Oh, what a hard lesson to learn and one we can all share. We are dangerously quick to divide the world into two camps, enemy and friend, and if someone is not a friend, we want to vanquish them right away. We want everything to go *our* way.

We want Jesus to be wielding a victorious sword. The disciples struggled to understand. When Jesus was arrested before his Crucifixion, one of his followers—Peter perhaps—drew a sword and cut off the ear of the high priest's slave. He's told to stop. "Put your sword back into its place," Jesus says, "for all those who take the sword will perish by the sword." Never were truer words spoken, no matter how often we don't want to listen.

Peace cannot come to the world without inner peace. Again and again, Jesus shows us how to gain that. To love our enemies, to forgive others, to forgive ourselves, to pray fervently as he did, even when he was being crucified to stop the whole thing . . . but no, he had to let go, to forgive, to love and go with the bigger story, the one that would make the biggest difference to us in our suffering, a resurrection that we could and would share. The message of a Messiah, who he is, turned out to be more amazing than anyone could have ever guessed.

Those who wield the sword die by the sword. There is a better, lovelier, holy way.

Reflections for Modern Living

- How do you look for and find inner peace?
- If Jesus gives us peace "not as the world gives it," where then would it be?
- Who are the peacemakers you have found or followed?
- What can you do when you're tempted to "take up the sword" in anger?

40

We Will All Learn

Clueless, struggling, trusting, and still looking for answers. I think of Gertrude Stein, who reportedly said on her deathbed, "What is the answer?" followed by, "In that case, what is the question?" Jesus, for us, is both the answer and the question. But as we've noted, when asked a question, he often responded with a question. Why? Because he wants us to grow, to seek, to never give up, to discover his goodness and own it. We need to ask questions of ourselves.

To go back to that story Jesus tells of the Pharisee and the tax collector uttering their own respective prayers, the Pharisee is full of self-congratulation. He thanks God that he is not like others, going through the list of "thieves, rogues, adulterers, even this tax collector," whereas the tax collector, beating his breast and looking up to heaven, feeling completely inadequate, simply asks for mercy. As Jesus points out, that's the right place to be. How uncomfortable it can be, and how right it is.

In *The Cloud of Unknowing*, one of the great works of Christian mysticism, written in Middle English back in the fourteenth century, the author asserts how it is in the profound act of *un*knowing that we can come to know the divine, and ourselves. The book, written by some anonymous soul, possibly a priest, possibly a monk, probes the mystery of faith. The

writer promotes the practice of contemplative prayer, or meditation, to let go of what we think we know. We find God when we give up all intellectual certitude and simply trust, like that tax collector. What a contrast to our current milieu when we seek notoriety—influence—by collecting more followers and friends on social media with our pronouncements and photos. "Friend" has become a verb with a quantifiable meaning. (Should we rewrite the lyrics to "What a Friend We Have in Jesus?")

Jesus knows how we can be more by simply being less. "All who exalt themselves will be humbled, but all who humble themselves will be exalted." Modern success in the world is to be an influencer. I can't imagine Jesus calling himself that. He's not trying to sell anything; he's not looking for bigger numbers. He's trying to sell us to ourselves.

Think of how few followers he had in his short lifetime, practicing his ministry in a cultural backwater. He couldn't have reached more than a few thousand. The biggest number comes when he takes pity on the crowd that has been following him and feeds some five thousand with only five loaves of bread and a few fishes (or was it also the compassion aroused in them that led them to share what they'd stashed away in satchels or cloaks?). After his resurrection there's another account of him appearing to five hundred. Still, it doesn't add up to a lot for a religion that is practiced by well over two billion people today, the largest faith practice in the world.

Right from the beginning the good word spread through the telling and retelling of the stories and messages we have explored here. In an era when few could read, long before printing was even possible, people came to Jesus by listening and learning. Jesus's words "Wherever two or three are gathered in my name, there I am with them" proved to be truer than anyone could suspect. He didn't write any books, he didn't craft some template for leadership that could be followed for millennium, he didn't build any buildings; he simply gave us this promise that when even just a few of us gathered together, in his name, he would be there and is there, whether it's on Zoom—could he have guessed at that?—online, by phone, or in person. When I immerse myself in Jesus, reading Scripture, reimaging a story, listening to a sermon, studying some commentary, I never feel alone. As different as we can be, even if we differ in our interpretations, we are one in the Lord.

As should be patently obvious, I am no biblical scholar or learned theologian, as much as I delight in learning from them. I am simply a guy who yearns to follow Jesus. The more I know, the less I know, and the more delight I take in learning. I can't get enough of it. This spiritual journey we are on goes on and on. During times of struggle, I can wonder if I've lost Jesus; at the same time, I know he has never lost me. In the Gospels we learn of and see Jesus's exasperation with his disciples. Will they ever get it? Will they ever learn, even his beloved Peter, who denied him three times before the Crucifixion? And yet . . . and yet . . . as we learn, especially in the book of Acts that follows the Gospels, they proved to be devoted, heroic, even willing to give their lives for the Lord.

May we all be lifelong learners. There's no stopping what we can do and who we can become. But then, we are always the Lord's.

REFLECTIONS FOR MODERN LIVING

- Do you ever read a verse of Scripture, scratch your head, and wonder what it's all about?
- Can you be comfortable with the notion that not knowing can lead to knowing?
- Who are you best spiritual teachers?
- How do you find the time and energy to trust in their wisdom?

Acknowledgments

So many people have helped me on my journey with Jesus: Mom and Dad, and those prayers he said every night at dinner; Sunday school teachers like Mrs. Clarke, who prayed aloud for us squirming kids; Rick Thyne, a passionate follower of the Way; our faith community at St. Michael's Church in New York; the Sunday school kids I taught and learned from; saints on the journey like Margaret Cotterell; ministers no longer with us like Fred Hill and Jeff Gill; the guests at our soup kitchen; colleagues at work such as Edward Grinnan, Amy Wong, and Jim Hinch; the writings of Richard Rohr; the podcasts *Hunger for Wholeness* and *The Bible for Normal People*; Christ Church Greenwich where I can call our son, Rev. Tim, Father; our grandkids Silas, Ricky, Mae, and Scott, who help me embrace the child within; prayer partners like Debbie Macomber and Mary Lou Carney; probing faith breakfasts with Jim Hilboldt, Scott Lethbridge, and David Straut; the men of St. Mike's; women who preach the Word and live it—thank you Mother Julie Hoplamazian and Mother Kate Flexer; the healing powers—bless you Dr. O'Connor, Dr. DiMango, and Dr. Feltheimer. Nurses India and Rivkah; the prayer ministry of Arlene Bullard; my EFM compatriots; the joy of singing in choir with John Cantrell; the Cabrini Shrine, thanks to Julia Attaway and the Majesta Chanters; learning spiritual direction through the Haden Institute; the everlasting sermons of Bill Coffin at Riverside Church (when I was a chorister there); the inspiring model of writer friends like Stacy Schiff, Brenda Wineapple, Will Schwalbe, and our book group led by beloved Robert Klitzman; my siblings Gioia, Howard, and Diane, who still teach me; more friends than I could possibly name, starting with Patti, Jorge, Ginny, Peggy, Fred and Fred, Steve (who introduced us to St. Mike's), Pam, Jeff, Ray, Gretchen, Richard, Yang, Eric, Katherine, Marc, Rodney, Joanne, F. Paul, and neighbors like Juliet, Jeff, Mary Alice, Robert, Annie, Eve and Alberto, and more.

All the above and countless others have been with me as I seek to "have life," as Jesus promises, "and have it more abundantly." This book would not have happened without the patience and guidance of my agent Bob Hostetler and editor Roma Maitlall. God bless 'em.

Author's Notes

Here are the biblical texts I refer to and quote from, chapter and verse. All are from the NRSV:

Chapter 1: The Samaritan woman at the well, John 4:1–42
Chapter 2: Parable of the Talents, Matthew 25:14–30
Chapter 3: Parable of the sheep and goats, Matthew 25:31–46
Chapter 4: Love for Enemies, Matthew 5:43–48
Chapter 5: The Wedding at Cana, John 2:1–11
Chapter 6: Twelve-year-old Jesus at the temple in Jerusalem, Luke 2:41–52; the temptation in the desert, Matthew 4:1–15 and Luke 4:1–13
Chapter 7: Parable of the workers in the vineyard, Matthew 20:1–6
Chapter 8: Jesus and the rich young man, Mark 10:17–27, Luke 18:18–30, and Matthew 19:16–26. Jesus looking at him and "loved him" is only in Mark (verse 21).
Chapter 9: The feeding of the five thousand is in all four gospels, Matthew 14:13–21, Mark 6:31–44, Luke 9:12–17, and John 6:1–4. For the feeding of the four thousand, go to Matthew 15:32–39 and Mark 8:1–9. Also, Luke 6:38: "Give, and it will be given to you."

Chapter 10: "Whoever comes to me and does not hate . . ." Luke 14:26

Chapter 11: The woman with the issue of blood, Matthew 9:20–22, Mark 5:25–34, and Luke 8:43–48. For other examples of Jesus healing on the sabbath, there is the woman crippled for eighteen years, Luke 13:10–17; a man with dropsy, Luke 14:1–6; and a man with a withered hand, Matthew 12:9–13, Mark 3:1–6, and Luke 6:6–11.

Chapter 12: Parable of the Pharisee and the Tax Collector, Luke 18:9–14

Chapter 13: Jesus tells us not to worry, Matthew 6:25–34

Chapter 14: The man with an Unclean Spirit, Mark 1:21–28; the house divided against itself, Mark 3:22–27; the man who lived among the tombs, Matthew 8:28–34, Mark 5:1–20, and Luke 8:26–39; "When the unclean spirit has gone out of a person . . ." Matthew 12:43–45

Chapter 15: Jesus welcomes the children, Matthew 19:13–15, Mark 10:13–16, and Luke 18:15–17. "Truly I tell you . . . Whoever welcomes one such child in my name welcomes me," Matthew 18:3–5.

Chapter 16: Jesus Heals a Paralytic, Matthew 9:2–3, Mark 2:1–12, and Luke 5:17–26

Chapter 17: Jesus asked about paying taxes, Matthew 17:24–27, Mark 12:13–17, and Luke 20:20–26; Jesus asked about divorce, Matthew 19:3–9 and Mark 10:2–9

Chapter 18: The shepherds at Christ's birth, Luke 2:8–20; Mary's says the Magnificat, Luke 1:46–55; wise men come from the East, Matthew 2:1–12; the flight into Egypt, Matthew 2;13–15; the slaughter of the innocents, Matthew 2:16–18; the trip home, Matthew 2:19–23

Chapter 19: Parable of the Sower, Matthew 13:1–23, Mark 4:1–20, and Luke 8:4–15

Chapter 20: The death and raising of Lazarus, John 11:1–44
Chapter 21: Nicodemus Visits Jesus, John 3:1–21; Nicodemus speaks up for Jesus, John 7:50–51; Nicodemus helps prepare Christ's body for burial, John 19:39–40; the woman who anointed Jesus, Matthew 26:6–13, Mark 14:3–9, John 12:1–8, and Luke 7:36–50
Chapter 22: Jesus on cleaning the cup, Matthew 23:26 and Luke 11:39; "All who exalt themselves will be humbled . . ." Matthew 23:12
Chapter 23: Parable of the Lost Sheep, Matthew 18:12–14 and Luke 15:1–7; Parable of the Lost Coin, Luke 15:8–10; Parable of the Prodigal and His Brother, Luke 15:11–32
Chapter 24: Jesus inviting the disciples to follow him, Matthew 4:18–22, Mark 1:16–20, Luke 5:1–11, and John 1:35–42; Jesus heals Peter's mother-in-law, Matthew 8:14–15, Mark 1:29–31, and Luke 4:38–39; the risen Jesus appears to the disciples as they're fishing, John 21:1–14; Peter briefly walks on water, Matthew 14:28–33; the Transfiguration, Matthew 17:1–8, Mark 9:2–8, and Luke 9:28–36; Jesus Washes the Disciples' Feet, John 13:1–9
Chapter 25: Jesus is the light of the world, John 8:12, and we are the light of the world, Matthew 5:14–16
Chapter 26: Jesus says, "And if your right hand causes you to sin . . ." in Matthew 5:29–30.
Chapter 27: Jesus speaks about pain and childbirth, John 16:21–22; "But about that day . . ." Matthew 24:36
Chapter 28: "Do not judge . . ." Matthew 7:1; "Do not condemn . . ." Luke 6:37–38
Chapter 29: "No one who puts a hand . . ." Luke 9:62; "Let the dead bury their own dead, but as for you . . ." Luke 9:60
Chapter 30: Healing the leper, Matthew 8:1–4; healing two blind men, Matthew 9:27–30; restoring the child to life, Luke 8:40–56

Chapter 31: The Syrophoenician woman, Mark 7:24–30.
Chapter 32: "Whoever loves father or mother more than me . . ." Matthew 10:37–39; twelve-year-old Jesus lingering behind at the temple in Jerusalem, Luke 2:41–52
Chapter 33: The unjust judge and the persistent widow, Luke 18:1–8; parable of the unshrunk cloth, Matthew 9:16 and Mark 2:21; the metaphor of new wine in old wineskins, Matthew 9:17, Mark 2:22, and Luke 5:37–38; parable of the shrewd manager, Luke 16:1–9
Chapter 34: "Where two or three are gathered in my name . . ." Matthew 18:20; "Let such a one be to you as a gentile . . ." Matthew 18:17; "Truly I tell you, whatever you bind on earth . . ." Matthew 18:18; "two by two," Mark 6:7–13 and Luke 10:1–2
Chapter 35: "I am the way . . ." John 14:6; overturning the tables in the temple, Matthew 21:12–17, Mark 11:15–18, Luke 19:45–48, and John 2:13–16 (with slight variations, and possibly more than one occasion); "Father, if you are willing, remove this cup . . ." Luke 22:42
Chapter 36: "You see all these, do you not?" Matthew 24:2; "You know that after two days . . ." Matthew 26:2; "For nation will rise against nation . . ." Matthew 24:7, Mark 13:8, and Luke 21:10; "Then they will hand you over to be tortured . . ." Matthew 24:9; "And this good news of the kingdom . . ." Matthew 24:14; "When you see the desolating sacrilege . . . nursing infants," Matthew 24:15–19; ". . . of the elect those days will be cut short," Matthew 24:22; "Immediately after the suffering of those days . . ." Matthew 24:29–31; "Truly I tell you . . ." Matthew 24:34
Chapter 37: "The Son of Man is going to be betrayed . . ." Matthew 17:22 and Mark 9:31; "This is my Son . . ." Matthew 17:5, Mark 9:7, and Luke 9:35; "They have taken away my Lord . . ." John 20:13; "Peace be with you," John 20:19;

doubting Thomas and Jesus, John 20:24–29; Jesus on the road to Emmaus, Luke 24:13–35

Chapter 38: The Parable of the Good Samaritan, Luke 10:25–37

Chapter 39: "For a child has been born for us . . ." Isaiah 9:6; "Blessed are the peacemakers . . ." Matthew 5:9; "Peace I leave with you . . ." John 14:27; "But who do you say that I am?" Matthew 16:15–16, Mark 8:29, and Luke 9:20; "Get behind me, Satan!" Matthew 16:23 and Mark 8:33; "Put your sword back into its place . . ." Matthew 26:52

Chapter 40: Parable of the Pharisee and the Tax Collector, Luke 18:9–14